Impressum:

Fritz Dominik Buri
From guests to friends
„The 1x1's personal guests loyality

Avalible at : Amazon
Release Date : February 2014
Pages : 92
Language : English
Cover designed: Fritz Dominik Buri

ISBN Number :
ISBN-13: 978-1495931956

© Copyright : Fritz Dominik Buri

Contents

A few words to the english version　　page 4

Preface or struck by lightning　　Page 5

The basic idea behind　　page 8

The only thing that disturbs is the guest　　page 12

Children and dogs knows exactly which restaurant they want　　page 19

A small favor desired　　page 23

Other questions lead to other considerations,　　page 29

The Pareto principle converted to the catering　　page 35

From imitators and other evildoers　　page 40

The necessary imagination　　page 44

Deliver what is desired!　　page 51

What we can learn from Steve Jobs　　page 55

People have desires!　　page 62

Provide service - day in, day out!　　page 67

Trivialities but important　　page 72

The employee has the word　　page 77

Let's summarize　　page 86

To say remains dear reader ....　　page 91

About the Author　　page 92

A few words to the English version

The incredible response of the german edition of "From guests to friends" has inspired me to write this English version, or should I say translate.

I know gastronomy is around the world a topic because everywhere people go in hotels and restaurants or bars to eat, to stay or just to meet friends and enjoy good times together.
And the original German version was also intended for the german-speaking countries, like for Switzerland Germany and Austria but the principles you will find in this rate encoder, can be applied to any restaurant business.
No matter where the place will be, people are all the same wherever you go, right?

Because, no matter where people are guests in a restaurant or hotel, this was in Europe, Asia or America, the principles apply to the whole world and will help any interested in and support him to build a better relationship with his guests and his part contribute to guest binding.

And I myself, who has been to many places around the world at home, know that I appreciate it when I am perceived as a guest and treated as a friend, even if I should never return to this place again, so my beautiful memories to be remember this place forever in my thoughts and I will always like to remind myself.
And I'm going to recommend this operation to my friends and everyone you know, when I know that you drive there or get in the holiday or business addresses in the region.

And the more people I reach with my books and I can help you to do things differently and maybe a bit better for himself and his guests and friends, now my friend, then I have indeed fulfilled my mission and I look me, rather have helped you readers can.

Wherever you may just be reading these lines, I wave to you and wish you and your loved ones a lot of fun in life and that you can contribute my lines, for a better understanding with your fellow employees and guests.

And now you loan back and let yourself be inspired "from guests to friends" comfort from.
Let's have a good time together you and me – we both?
Are you ready to start with me, so then we went ahead and practice some new and interesting behavior pattern for you and your business.

Preface or struck by lightning

First, I want you dear reader and dear reader, my thanks to say that you have chosen "from guests become friends" and thus to acquire this book.
This book is addressed to you, to you as an interested reader and reader and it designed to show you with simple methods you from your guests and friends make and how you can stand out with actions of the masses.

After all - where do you like to go out?
To where you are welcomed as a guest and gladly seen are!

Cooking shows and cookbooks abound and I look very much like Cooking shows and also study every now and again like new recipes a variety of cookbooks, this is simply because I like to cook and guests spoil, because food and drink were around since the dawn of time and quite sure, as we now know from history, even at the old Romans always a sign of joy and pleasure.
But something does not exist, namely books as a guide for caterers, books a successful guest loyalty, a targeted build a loyal and thus constantly recurring clientele and new guests.
Because, unfortunately, this has become a widespread fact that in many places farms who are struggling with sales decline and this partly end up in a bankruptcy for the corresponding operation ends.

So is precisely in this area, the targeted binding guests a huge Pent-up demand there and the idea for this book made me literally like a flash blindsided.
So I sat down and started to write down and it was really me easy to write this book, the ideas and lines shot me also literally by itself on the paper, respectively.
The keyboard.
It seems to me (even if only in retrospect) as before, as though this knowledge
the very long slumbered in me finally to the public, ie written be I have even performed operations for many years and tell you here so from my personal experience gained in daily contact with the guests and employees , you dear reader will therefore not bone dry just theory of mine to get read , but practical knowledge from which you most immediately and this can implement the same into action and ensure that you to your relationship their guests and employees throughout redefine .
And yet I have something detected during write this book, a deep sense of gratitude and joy in me, grateful, therefore, to give you my To be able to share experiences on their way to new insights and Insights.
And joy, the writing is so easily passed from hand to me, had as already mentioned, and I have the impression that this book was already be written long , as if an inner voice whispers to you in the ear ,na at last you got it , good boy.

It is my heartfelt wish you with this present book, a real benefits and added value for yourself and give your company and convey can, like a gift to a good old friend.

An added value also for your guests and their employees, just all the people with whom you are in contact every day and the fact that this after reading Book a couple of things will see with different eyes (I am convinced) go and build and a new type of bond to be.

The methods of the guest binding works, I have you applied yourself, every applied day and, as one might expect of the working methods and may achieve the results desired.
And this is not just a day, no permanent because you want to finally no storm break in a teacup over the fence, you have bought this book and read it is because you want to permanently change something and I am as an author you guilty you for your time and effort and money, a real benefit provide.
This because of the following:
In my many years as a restaurateur, a coach and a private citizen, I have the made experience that only long-term based on respect, respect and appreciation based relationships guarantee a real benefit for those involved.
And yet I would like to mention at this point that for an important quintessence a long-term success in any industry is essential:
Always ensure a win win situation for all sides, all pages of working with you to benefit, there are only winners and no losers in this game.

Short-term successes are like lies and these are known to have short legs.

Just as for me, sustainability and durability of two important values in represent my life, so shall also the book for you and your company provide durability and long life so that you, your guests and employees find themselves in a win win situation

As for food, we have to it with people of all countries and races do and I think that's exactly what makes this profession, this diversity
Where else, I ask you, you can contribute as much to the understanding as in the restaurant business, if not where else if you please!
But enough said, let us go together to work, so They too have bought this book.
So let's now common to tread this path from your guests
To make friends, do you agree?

Look at it from the side, your fixed costs you one way or another, whether your business now is full or empty and the staff and the power company, you can not
say, "Sorry folks, it was just a bad month and then for you this Month nothing in it, but we are confident that it will get better soon! "

And nothing, even excuses or justifications do not change the fact that only a visit from guests who eat with you and drink it ensure that an exchange of money takes place.
And, neither you nor your staff are rewarded for your effort.

In this book I will provide you with valuable information, and what I say based on my experience, not based on any theory, which has come up with anyone in a stunning ivory tower.
You see, I know my way around and have paid my dues.
Benefit from my experience and save yourself unnecessary expense and Investment, because why make all learn by experience, if someone else for you has already been collected and made his experience and now you passes.
Remember, each of us have to buy the price, the price to get the best in his district and when you want to climb the top of the hill, you have to do everything that is needed to get up to the top, there's no abbreviation.

Many people not only reach your goals, therefore, because they are doing what they should not do really, they know what to do, but they just do it not.
Do what you need to do and then enjoy the success, but you must do whatever is necessary to reach where they want.

Then I would say we get started ☺

Sincerely

Your Dominik Fritz Buri

The basic idea behind

Let us now therefore ran the nitty-gritty.
We live in a fast paced, new products and services emerge almost every day, much is useful and some products are not likely and therefore just as quickly disappear from the market again as they appeared.

Much of what seemed unthinkable a few decades ago and as Science Fiction was dismissed, today is reality and what was not regarded as normal, was anyway pushed aside.
And what is considered normal, it means that the masses going on in this way and is, but if the masses are normal, that does not mean that this is also good, it's just normal because all make it so.
Because we know nothing else and therefore makes it as one of the sets in the manner of "all do it that way" or "we have always done so, as everyone else ".
Were until a few years ago a patriarchal leadership style than normal, the Chief orders and have to knuckle down and followed the instructions to afford, so a lot has changed in this regard, thank God.
And even with this kind of leadership one has noticed that this was the normal Leadership style of this period was, but that this is so not the best leadership style is, no one questioned it's the way it is and that's that.

As already mentioned, we are living through a moment of social change through all Layers goes.
Tried and tested is accepted for more than irrefutable and people begin to draw on their own thoughts and questioning systems and processes.
Not only technologically new approaches are in demand and on the rise, no well
the people themselves begin to ask questions, questions about the meaning of life, and they are looking for answers, responses for a better understanding between each other.
An interested employee wants to know today what's on and wants OPERATION OF therefore be informed and involved, but employees spend a large proportion of their time in business.
And so it is understandable that an employee perceived and wants to be respected, that a boss trusts him and also skills acknowledges, because no one really likes paternalism, we are always with want to do adult men, and they also treated accordingly and be perceived.

On the other hand, guests demanding and offer wider become, they expect for their money more than just food and drink served to get, the visit to the restaurant to be a ritual.
Formerly served hotels and restaurants mainly for the purpose of due eat like drink and sleep to meet basic needs, there is also a rapid change happen.
Wellness is the buzzword, and hardly wanted a hotel and could not be afford this trend not to join.

Yes, the guest of today has become more demanding and picky and he can allow themselves to be picky, because even in small villages is the offer at restaurants around not even to write greatly from an oversupply.
So the paying guest is spoiled for choice and what makes someone the agony has the choice?
Right, he goes there where he - in his eyes - the best value services receives, why settle for less when you get more for your money.

If we have followed here the development in recent decades, as we see that the gastronomic experience has arrived, the needs of young people changed over the course of time, just in a restaurant or bar to go for a drink was suddenly no longer cool, Halli Galli fun entertainment and other concepts were needed.

However, many of these concepts have disappeared again, the rapid money was made by the operators and on these concepts were also designed to skim right in one to two years and then something new.
With other words, start something new and funny to gotta meet the needs
They were followed on the foot of the kebab and fast food stalls in the last ten years mushroomed out of the ground and partly classical catering the water and thus the lunch guests ate away.
But even here, we are in another chapter later in this book respond to this issue yet and I'll teach you how to also as can compete by responding flexibly.

Companies like Migros and Coop (like Wal Mart) have recognized that children customers of tomorrow and that children can be very stubborn when they want something.
And yes, if you are a reader, even the parents of children, then know You what I'm writing here, children aged six to twelve years can be right little buggers when they put something in the head have that they want.
Also in the restaurant business are children a target group which many far too little
Pay attention and I'll show you in another chapter, that children can invigorate your business with new customers quite a bit.

But we come back to the basic idea has led me to to write this book.
The rapid change has not just restricted to the catering and many Restaurateurs have missed it, sorry if I write it like that, but they have it slept the signs of the times in order to recognize new flexible enough to respond to needs and situations.
Partially had long-established businesses close their doors forever because they did not recognize the signs of time or were not ready to face the new to face challenges.
My book should serve you, the readers to give him new ideas, other and indeed to make smart questions, things to question and re-to reconsider.
And stop yourself from successful companies and we read again and again that even they are struggling to maintain sales and guests can order their maintain position in the market and to maintain it.

What is the reason for this?
Do people less money than before?
Walking people often eat out less than before?
Part like these reasons have their place, but these are not the true reasons for the fall!
In a static model, people have much more money to spend than before.
Is it then in the end even on the mobility?
No, people are now more mobile than ever before in the history of
Humanity, in many cities and urban areas is the public transport network
excellent expanded to weekdays and weekends to two clock
to come out at night to go home, you want to have a nice drink and the
Save search of parking stress.
What is the decline in customer numbers then look?

If it is not to be sought in the outside, then where?
Inside !
Exactly, in the interior that is in the restaurant business, respectively . hotels and restaurants itself
A study in Austria from 2010 was exactly the above questions the reason to go to find out what and what the reasons for the guests jerk transition are !
Thousands of hotels and restaurants were tested anonymously by saw to it whether the service operates an active sale, welcoming guests friendly and were also adopted again , test calls are made to test whether you receive competent advice on the phone .
The result was sobering:
In half of the tested plants no active sale and was a operated up selling to mention .
At the seventy percent could make over the phone no precise information as their opening times and are forty percent could not tell whether it is a Banquet had documentation or when the boss or manager in the operating will be present.
Facts of truth – unfortenally.

There were other points listed in this study all of them as no good testimony for the catering could be used.

This leads us to the following conclusion:
In operation, it is the same as with an individual who wants to be a Achieve business (operation) other results in the outside (guests), must (operation) held a change only in the interior, before this change in the outer visible improvement, bringing different results.

Also for these successful restaurateurs I still do in my book, to consider and find out what is successful and what with the host or owner of the largest and most sales take and then, I know first time, where I earn money with the company to strengthen this area.

Maybe you say the term the Pareto principle something after the Italians Pareto named.

It's all about the 80/20 rule.

For the professional that would mean that we with our twenty percent customers derive eighty percent of our sales, we at twenty percent of our hotel room eighty percent of sales in the generate nights etc.

This rule has been found by this gentleman, by his observations and calculations made for years on end, just the one company, with twenty percent of its best customers eighty percent sales generates, that Twenty percent of the sales force eighty percent of the generate total revenues of the sales force.

How can you apply this 80/20 rule for your company I will tell you in another chapter in this book.

It was precisely this principle, I am approached this book with the restaurant and hotel business and its employees only an internal change trigger, so then a visible external change, respectively.

Improvement occurs.

If you now think that this is a difficult task, then I can calm down dear reader.

All you need is the desire to want to change something, an open spirits and attitude ... last, something good will.

With these three properties, you have already done half the distance.

For the other half of the way I am your companion, agrees.

For if I have done that, then I am convinced that you are getting the can, because the desire for change is in them, because otherwise you would not bought this book.

So we continue on our way to the next chapter.

So, let's go ahead, right buddy?

The only thing that disturbs the guest is

Yes , this finding I had to do already , namely that I inopportune come and thus am also undesirable.
If I 'm undesirable as a guest, why then you close your shop not just from a sign hanging out , we have closed and the matter is ate and not a guest needs to stay within the operation again , come here
I never recover, because here I am unwanted.
Oh, how life would be nice if only the work would not and with the work of all the annoying guests with their small or big wishes.
If you have this setting or an employee in their operation on paying clientele is released , I would recommend at this point, quickly to change jobs and industry.
But even in another industry , we always have to do it with people and no man can survive on its own.
In another industry you are there perhaps with other customers and other wishes and concerns have to do , but can also in other industries some customers just now simply times be annoying or asking for something over normal parameters beyond - and now , so goes under the world.
Not at all .

But on the whole consideration, the basic idea is already wrong , because where
no one is, can also annoy or stress No one , really .
So no matter, we are always dealing with people, even in private life we have
dealing with people who want something from us , and if it's only the waste is the partner expects us to take him outside.
And it will continue playing no matter if it is the kebab shop around the corner or the Bistro at the mall , or even a hotel, all of these modes and each other company lives the fact that it has customers with whom it in exchange stands , visit the catering as guests of the operation .
Because - no guests = no sales and no sales means = no merit .
In order to survive we need the guests eat and drink to us and or come to stay , so our services for money to complete take and they expect in return appropriate treatment and Operation, brings as a guest and as the person the money and the staff and the owner ensures the existence .
Thus is the cycle of the economy.

I have nothing that I can trade for money, so I would not earn revenue, no more and no less.
I know some people in the catering well believe their reward is of paid love God or the boss has a rich uncle or have otherwise which dubious ideas where and what their reward is paid.
You get your reward from the guest and therefore ensure you make this your guest always again and especially love to you is to take out the long-term operation alive
to obtain.
And from no one else as the guests that went into your hotel oder restaurant, thers is no rich dad or uncle or maybe god that paid your checks.

You may think that I am exaggerating a bit at the moment, but I can give you assure you that I've seen people in the restaurant business who really thought their reward would be paid from somewhere, where no matter because as long as the wage is
, these people get interested and not where the money comes, the main thing it is how and where does not matter.
No, matter is not that and you as a business owner should do this time your clearly lead fishing Presented in mind, where their salary comes.
Some will perhaps look surprised, but these employees will have it then grasped and tear on the belt accordingly.
Some people just have to get out of their dreams and make clear how the circulation of the economy works and before logging in as the boss and employers also do not push, but it helps you in the employees for a to provide better understanding and less complaining when the store times again is packed.

Even an employee trades his time for money, working at the hotel as XY and so many hours in a month and get paid in return for his
Hours at the end of the month his paycheck.
Or you know someone who works for free or a company's products or services away from an impulse of kindness and mercy out?
Probably not and why is that so?
Because our society, that is our economic system is so constructed that you provide a value for the receipt of products or services must, therefore money.
Thus, a catering company needs so that it can survive, in the guest the operation come to eat and drink.

So we see we have always and everywhere to do it with and without people
People and paying customers is not much and also a hotel or restaurant must make some sales if it has open to all its
Obligations to comply, since the end of the month will not only employees his wages, as well as the power plant, the suppliers and all others want see cash.
The simple rule is: No guest = no sales.

Not every day is a peak day and from some experience I know that you also occasionally has low-selling days, but should this weak sales
Days do not become a permanent condition otherwise then go the doors for a longer period of time.
And the consequence of this, the staff must be better or worse after look for a new job, not matter how long they have worked in the operation and which had reigned for a great working atmosphere but when the oven is off, then he made.
And the hotelier and restaurateur himself?
Often these people are what often facing a financial disaster ends in a bankruptcy.
This need not be, and the host or the hotel owner had the whole thing completely determined otherwise presented as the mess he has at the end in front of him.

So the guest is not a factor which interferes with , but a person who assists in favor to ensure that there is no disaster , so each guest should he thoughjust drinking a coffee with kindness and operated carefully.

Basically, logically you will answer me now and this should be also think, but unfortunately that is not the case as you have already mentioned in the study from Austria have seen .

Because if several employees would be aware of where their pay comes and
ultimately pays for their paycheck, then would the result of the study been very different.

By the way, in Germany and in Switzerland, the results would be similar been stored as in Austria .

But unfortunately, one might think, this clouded vision prevails only in the employees, and the hosts would whistle in another pipe - far from it!

On a visit to a restaurant at lunchtime, and I were a another guest the only two people who ate some lunch , except us two had two people in the restaurant each having only a cup of coffee drank.

So not exactly what could be described as a full house for lunch.

When I asked (the host sat in the pub and filled a crossword puzzle off) as he was satisfied , he replied , " I 'm satisfied with how it runs !"

Aha , I thought , interesting for two sold lunch and two coffees .

About three months later, for I said back at the restaurant over and saw a board in front of the entrance are closed until further notice I read on the panel.

Further explanations are unnecessary in this context.

Guests are customers and flush money into the coffers of the company all the more survival to secure the company's sales and guests go back, this is a first warning sign that something should be changed and quickly.

Otherwise, it means then suddenly in front of the entrance door also until further notice closed.

So we scare our paying guests through an unfriendly demeanor, bad food, inattention or lack of hygiene so we must not be surprised if the number of guests decreases more and more.

Since no whining, and the error in the outside helps to look for, in politics or that the economic crisis is to blame, that the operation has to fight.

Because there are successful catering company which are always well attended and of whom are no words of complaining.

Look around you and observe the successful companies in the Industry, what make this different from the mass so that they are so successful.

And you will find that successful companies do differently, they value the friendliness and courtesy and give the guest a feeling you're welcome to me what can I do for you dear guest to you the
To make stay in our home as comfortable as possible.

With exactly this attitude and perspective towards the customer should successful restaurants and hotels to work and give the guest the feeling you are important to me and welcome, so a lived hospitality.
This will cost you no money to serve only the readiness for operation in the Word serve the word which serve means nothing other than to fulfill wishes for the welfare of others.

So always wear the idea of well-being for your guests in their efforts upright and make sure their staff also ensure that these have understood this, and indeed that this would have all understood both the Cuisine as well as the service, the reception and the floor - in short, all employees in the company, this attitude should put on the day and if a of which not one of them is able or willing , then you should stay away from this employees separate, because he or she is their company and the reputation of the House harm.
And I think you want and can not afford a host or a hotel owner?
Employees on board have to bring you more harm than good.

And here's a note for all the people who have direct contact with the host has, so be on the front!

« They represent the company to outside the guest and his Companions. »

Is the food even cold or has a wrong side dish delivered, you can quickly make up for with kindness and charm again.
On the other hand, the best food and the best wine is rude and with a served and performed lewd behavior, the guest receives the impression that I and my guests are here probably not welcome and he and his guests think twice if they this hotel or restaurant one more time will visit

The mind game does not end at this point and goes even further.
The guest and his companions were scared , will not say , Mr. Miller of Restaurant X was rude and sloppy, or Miss Huber Hotel K was snippy and cranky and impersonal.
Guests will say the following to their friends and acquaintances ;
" The X restaurant, I can not recommend and advise urgently by a isit "or" Like the hotel K , since you want to invite us no pleasure in a another hotel but not in K , because as we have very bad experience made, we prefer to go to the Greeks eat because the service is friendly and courteous "
So you see, it does not mean Mr. Meier or Miss Huber , no, it means you Operation is representative of the offending employees affected in the drawn public and that only because an employee at the front has behaved unprofessionally .

Grumpy and disgruntled employees and bosses have nothing on the front lost, they harm than good to the company longer, they should be because of me the wine cellar clean up because they scare at least not paying guests.

Consider and apply the following into account.
Negative news travels faster than positive and from the Reason to mention most people more negative than positive when it comes to his experience with other people and acquaintances to pass.

A simple question for you?

Can you afford that two hundred fifty (250) persons ill of your operation and talk no longer come and stay with you?
You will now ask what this has to do with two hundred and fifty in number and how this is to be understood?

Well, calculations have shown that the average person (ie not a professional or person from public life), on average, until his forty-fifth year of life has two hundred and fifty people from his Schooling, training, points which he already held, clubs hobbies etc.
This number is not to be written just arbitrary, but is based on calculations have been made that a person in the course of his life knows until the age of forty-five so many people, whether man or woman.
Now I ask you, then, you can use it as a hotelier or restaurateur permit with two hundred and fifty persons to be on a war footing, just because an employee their Guest has scared away by his way?
I do know the answer to, and it also establishes you can not this do

Perhaps you have never seen the whole thing from this side, then it is well and at the time, sometimes about worrying to realize that only have a single host can be sufficient (in theory) that due to this score two hundred and fifty persons not or no longer in your operating come.
Due to this fact you are your guest it from a different light see and it would not hurt to the staff, this fact to be informed, so that each individual can make his thoughts and is aware of what he impact on the company and so directly on his work takes.

For what it uses huge amounts in advertising stuck to for expensive ads in Newspaper to guests frequency boost, people come into their operations due to their advertising, gain a negative impression and after this first visit did not come back.
Then even the most sophisticated advertising measure was literally for the cat and you would be that you have invested into advertising with the money for the holidays ridden and a few nice days have indulged.
You would have had more of it.

What does it take to have a successful career?
Passion and personal commitment and a willingness to his job after to want to run the best of our knowledge and belief at the guest a best possible benefits to offer.
People who do not apply for some reason this willingness can or want, it is perhaps advisable to make some thought to the industry and to change the metier.

After all, it does not make much sense, his precious time with things and activities spend the no fun and personal joy.
Such people do neither themselves nor their work environment happy because who already enjoys working with colleagues listless perform their work and only on hope to somehow get through another month and its content to get.

Therefore, the guest is not a nuisance and not a necessary evil, _unless you look at your paycheck as well as a necessary evil_, but I think now rather less, because money is the oil in the engine of the economy.

Show and let you know their guests and realize that you are in their company like to be seen and deliver more than is expected of you, then your also flourishing business and you need over decliners numbers and guests not to worry.
People meet people were they're welcome, give it to your customers and you, your staffmembers and the guests are satisfided about it.
It's easy, istn't it?

Personal notes and implementation points:

1. _____

_____

_____

2. _____

_____

_____

3. _____

_____

_____

4. _____

_____

_____

5. _____

_____

_____

Children and dogs knows exactly which restaurant they want!

Do you have children and dogs?
Those that even children have to know that these sometimes quite beautiful can be buggers when it comes to getting what they want.
They know exactly how and what they need to do to get to their destination, because they know I'm stubborn long enough then I get what I want and Mami or Daddy will yield.

As mentioned elsewhere, this also companies like Coop or Migros (names of shops chain) recognized this and use it for their sales strategy.
If the mother or father shopping at these retailers, they get always playing cards or other small items for their children, just things for the may be interested in children and collect and each other so that can swap and trade.
And this goes so far that in the children a real run on this article takes place (because kids love to collect, exchange and play) and with exactly this knowledge work companies, as it is called but, with bacon begins to mice.
Parents are therefore refrain from another dealer shop (although there they also get the same products and maybe even cheaper) but they know exactly the first when they get home is, the kids want asking them whether they have their coveted barter it. And alas, this is not the case, then go off the allegations, why did not you you know now, I will ...

What we learn from this?

Children are to get small egotist when it comes to what they want.
What does that mean for the catering industry and how can we know this for us use?
If you are like me grew up in the countryside and the village butcher shop had, then there was every time you visit a slice of sausage and that was just for us freshly cut from the butcher and handed over to us.
At that moment we felt like kings and because children as often as possible would like to feel like little kings, they are with an ally the person to be them feel the greatest, has given.
I would have loved to gone there every day with my mother to the butcher shop, waiting for the moment to my big appearance comes.

I was in one of my businesses an affiliated bakery and then went to the children by the hand, taking with them to the store and there they were somewhat choose and of course snacking same.
But the little ones have their gift only want to show their parents and went so back to her place, she proudly showed them then what they had chosen.
The parents were happy for your children and the children, now they felt like little kings, for they might with the boss personally to the store to get pick something.

Many mothers or parents told me that their children literally burn it in come to our operation and so they had to come easy, just have the because little ones, they would not have done it, a cry went out and they would be would have sulked all day. Do you remember what I have written to you at the beginning, children know exactly what they want and if they still get the feeling of a little king to be or princess, then they have a loyal ally found.

This principle can also be applied to the way dog owners.

For two reasons:
1 Dog owners will appreciate it if their four-legged friends are just as happy seen
be like the master or mistress itself
2 Appreciate it dog owners when their pets (especially in summertime) for free and without being a bowl of cold water provide.

In my businesses I have always seen that the dogs a bowl was put down with cold water and the animals themselves would value this as well as its owner.
Similarly, there was for the four-legged either a dog biscuit or a small piece Chocolate, depending on the agreement with the owner (dogs love chocolate).

Dogs and children have something in common:
Both dogs and kids know where there are sweets and they forget do not.
As I said, the dog got fresh addition to his bowl of cold water still a treat and the kids also got something sweet and where they want again with her master / mistress or mother / father down again: right, where they get their treats and sweets.

Also of dog owners I often got to hear that she evening on their walkies tour came to me because her dog straight on our operations is fed controls.
Or they let the dog run free, so this was usually quite a few minutes before his master or mistress in operation.
I am neither on the dog, respectively, on the child came, but as a dog owner I appreciate those little touches in a restaurant or hotel.
And the children?
Now that I remind myself of my childhood back and put myself in the Location of a child and how it must feel to them and parents expect these little touches that let their youngsters to be part of, high of.
As the host, you need to begin their customers and their wishes to exactly observe and ask yourself questions as you to offer their services to better can.

You see, these were just two of many examples how to use simple opportunities and financial expenditure without an added value for your customers provide.

This is relationship marketing at its finest.

It's about the experience, not the cup of water or the sweetness of the child, be but rather perceived as a guest, that he in our house is welcome.
Give your guests so the feeling of importance and of experience.

Again, you should consider the following:
Dog owners know again other dog owners as well as parents with children again to know other parents with children and they are positive about you and Your operation and talk to advertise for you and your company for free.
As I said, with bacon begins to mice or in other words, customer loyalty and acquiring new customers can be easy with the right methods.

The best thing is if you even play around with it and thereby make your own observations and experiences.
The recipe for this is: Just do it.

Personal notes and implementation points:

1. _____

_____

_____

2. _____

_____

_____

3. _____

_____

_____

4. _____

_____

_____

5. _____

_____

_____

A trifle complacent or for what you want to be known?

Little things often make a big difference from, or before the harvest can be retracted, must be sown!
Ask any farmer if he can harvest his wheat times without first sow?
He will look at you with big eyes and think that you are still sane, because he is wondering know each child to that first you must sow something afterwards to reap.
What in agriculture has its validity, also in the restaurant business in connection with the guest binding its validity.
Before you can reap (new guests) must first sow (action).

This is only logical to say now many, but if it is logical, why do it because so few.
Just as I know you kids and dogs in the preceding chapter precisely in which restaurant they want to have described, I have also sown there only before I could harvest, so a guest loyalty and New Guests at my farm could bind.

So as you can sow focused in catering to a to be able to count corresponding harvest I want you here to a few examples illustrate.
If you have guests who drink a glass of wine with you and chat want, but want to eat anything, then you can serve them some bread and cheese at no charge.
Also, this gesture is taken by your guests thanking note.
In 90% of cases I have seen that the result of this little attention guests getting hungry, because now were her taste - and stomach nerves been stimulated because the cheese has tasted them and so you order again
Wine and this time even a cheese and meat plate with this, so they chat drink and snack from the plate.
So let's now the bill new!
Originally wanted a few guests a glass of wine with you and entertain and chat with each other

Then you have served them free some cheese and bread, what their guests have taken note of thanks, again the taste buds of Guest has suggested and it has caused out to order a cheese plate.
And they ordered again after wine and even one or two bottles water.
From the originally planned francs or € 20 for a glass of wine were on end by re-order more wine and water and a cheese plate at the end francs or Euro 50 or more. (or dollars in this case.)
And all that just because you have first sown and from some cheese and bread have enough free wine.

a guest in your coffee or espresso ordered, then serve a glass of water with to free and something sweet.
But here, you will stand out from the crowd and do not serve a small piece of chocolate from the offering of the wholesalers, the best you can serve to coffee tea or a hot milk drink best homemade pastries.
Something that has the note of her house and not something that everyone has, you stand out so from the crowd.

And that costs you nothing, but brings a very large effect.

And this was mass you can come up with a homemade pastry take off
And who knows, maybe the a homemade pastries develop you serve the drinks become a true bestseller because the guests their homemade pastries house love.
Then offer this also on sale at 100 or 200 gram units in a beautiful packing (small little bag) with beautiful ribbon and you have already found a new source of income and opened.

Always remember the little things that make the difference and all the Advice I have betrayed you so far, you cost little money but bring a large positive response for your home and yourself.

Familiarize yourself now on the following question thoughts!

<u>For what or for what you and your company in the public want to be known</u>

What is or should their so-called USP (unique selling product) unique be selling product and bringing their guests and you identify and what you want to be perceived by the public and in the media!

Let's make an example to better illustrate that each of them knows.

The Confiserie Sprüngli in Zurich is world famous (and that is really so) for their Luxemburgerli they export to the world beyond.
This specialty is available all over the world and not just in Zurich alone with this product, the Confiserie Sprüngli has other products on offer but makes Sprüngli per year multi-million sales.
(And those things are pretty damn tasty).
If the name Sprüngli falls, then people automatically think Luxemburgerli without requiring them to be mentioned.
This should be in order to be clear an example of what you as a unique can look at selling the product and be what you known to the public wants.

Another example:
In ATTINGHAUSEN (place in the canton of Uri in Switzerland) there is a restaurant that far are known about the canton's borders for its chicken in a basket (Chicken in Basket) and the restaurant is partly joking half the chicken factory called, for the simple reason because this is their specialty and they have so many of them sale.

Therefore you considering for what your house will be known.
Are you thinking quietly something big and bold that does not need just as in the case be the Luxemburgerli world, but certainly far beyond the cantonal border addition.

Or you know the story of Colonel Sanders and his recipe, which was the basis for the later Kentucky Fried Chicken chain.
He had an idea and realized this.

The finding does not get right to the point they need good ideas sometimes a certain amount of time so that they can mature.
It may be that they fully or just the idea of the morning shower before going to sleep, important is simply that you have these thoughts and write down inspirations.
This is also the reason why I always have a notepad next to my Have bedside when the idea comes, I can these key words write to sift through my notes the next morning u, immediately to know what it was.
For inspiration have the habit of quietly to come and also in ,oments where we least expect it, we do not respond, disappear she so quietly as they came.
And it would be a real shame if you overtake the big idea and you miss it write them down and not remember the next morning it can.

But you can also ask their employees and in their considerations involve for what will be known to her house to the public and if a employee has the bright idea, you should give him or her an appropriate give reward.
You hit two birds with one stone:

1 Thinking and their employees make also thoughts and thereby create a brainstorming or an employee provides them an important Note, if there are multiple people come to think about something more solutions to the fore.
2 Appreciate it employees when they are asked for their opinion and you show their employees with this action that you to their opinion are interested, then employees feel actively involved in the action.

If you have found out for what their operation is to be known in the future, then make their message even known, let your website visitors know this, on the menus on the e mail signature to your facebook account etc.
Easy operation on all channels you communicated with the outside, because you
can have the best product or service have if nobody knows is set or in the knowledge, you will be able to generate no demand.

An example of mine:
On my business cards on the website and e mail signature I've looked everywhere my so-called "elevator pitch" sat down.
An elevator pitch, so a "lift hanger" is a message in a explains sentence what you do and your counterpart has any idea of their product or service.

My elevator pitch is as follows:
I am aware that I restaurateurs and hoteliers within 30 to improved days, measurable results contribute.

What is your elevator pitch for your company ?

If anyone reading this sentence, then he knows the same, aha Dominik Fritz Buri helps restaurateurs and hoteliers to better results within a month.
A one sentence is said everything important.

It's about standing out from the crowd and their uniqueness highlight what can you expect customer and guest with them where he otherwise nowhere receives.
What is their uniqueness!
"If you always do what everyone else is doing well, then you will always get what others receive too! "
So whether you have the courage and inspiration of new ways of customer acquisition to.
As you have seen and read all my tips are quickly and without great effort to implement, but you must do it and how I them in the Introduction've written, all you need is an open mind new ideas and perspectives to open.
The best business idea rotted on their hard drive or in her desk if you do not start and get into action and start their ideas to implement.

Catch prefer to imperfect than that you wait for the perfect plan and it never even come into action because their plan is not perfect.
Begin to observe how their new activities and actions at make their guests and customers felt, polish and refine as you might and there a little, test and then watch again until the desired results have you want.
And with all the here presented by me in this book measures to Guest loyalty you can test the reactions immediately on site.
In the example with the homemade biscuits and a glass of water for coffee or espresso, available or their employees receive immediate feedback from their guests.
Oh a homemade pastry and a glass of water, but this is nice and aware of them, thank you.
Oh, a pastry, I love pastries thank you.

Or in the case of the wine.
Wow, this is but mindful of them, thank you very much.

Or in the case of homemade pastry house, it may be that at this a real sales hit developed so as Luxemburgerli for confectionery Sprüngli are.
But you become so only find out if you tried it and made have, because you can lose nothing of it but in turn very much win.
If I give you the advice to consider for what their house should be known, I mean, to think what you are given from the currently can making opportunities and premises.
This allows you to get quick results and reactions, you must comply with the work resources that are available to them.
What you can implement immediately and without much effort now to their to give the required operating direction change wherever you want.
So do not you think, even if I only once, then ...... no, you can now use to availability infrastructure to implement staff.

Take your time in considering and as already mentioned, it may be that you need a few days until you have the right idea for their operation (or their partner or any of its employees) is important to have the knowledge that you want to change something.

And you bought this book with the idea to make a change because this book is intended to serve as their inspiration and guide, you have this book with the intention, I look a look and read it again, then it will give them be no great benefit and nothing will change.
It will only change something if you yourself made a strong decision have, yes I want and now I change something, not tomorrow or in a year.
No NOW and TODAY

The 72-hour rule, you should make it a habit!
Research has shown that people who, within 72 hours after they have made a decision to come into action, their projects and also run and pull tasks.

After that 72 hours after the determination, the probability is small that you ever start, let the idea fall back and realize the Ideas never.
Therefore it is important to get into the action, even if it's only the first notes and thoughts are that you begin to write down.
I know as a host and hotelier you have each day to my ears, but it is important also to take the time to work on their projects, because you are the captain of their operation and must always act with foresight.
Push less important things aside or delegate this to be the to devote their attention to more important things.

When I had the idea for this book, I'll be sat down and have started to write, pushed aside other things and me only times the devoted to writing this book.

For me is the 72-hour rule very well be a term and if I do not so had started, I would have the next day again had other things the would have stopped me to devote myself to this book.
And within three four days, I would still know in my Thoughts, you do want to start to write this book but would also again found other things which I had dedicated myself, just not this book.

The whole life is a series of decisions and the sum our choices determines the life we lead.
If I where I do not want to change something with the results in a range 'm satisfied, then I think about how and what results I want in this have range.
So what I want instead of what I no longer want to leave or not have, over to what I want.
More on this in the next chapter.

So what I want instead of what I no longer want to leave or not have, over to what I want.
This chapter, I would like to end with a quote from Henry Ford that I repeatedly call into consciousness when I look at and think about a project make their realization.ore on this in the next chapter.

"Whether you think being able to do something or not does not matter, you have to both cases right"

Personal notes and implementation points:

1. _____

   _____

   _____

2. _____

   _____

   _____

3. _____

   _____

   _____

4. _____

   _____

   _____

5. _____

   _____

   _____

Other questions lead to other considerations

Issues control our focus!
Do we have the same questions circling our thoughts always at the same And need to change things around this or we should start the rest of us to ask questions.
I call these questions the cunning questions which we then clever answers lead.

In the previous chapter, you've seen what thoughts you should be as their operation should be perceived by the public and for which you want to be known.
In a further step, you should consider what type of clientele you want to appeal, you have the clientele you want or you want a appeal to other customers in the future.
If so, then consider switching to the customer base for you in the future in their operation want to have.

And another question is: What benefits do you want to offer their guests?
Guests have an expectation when they come to them in the operation, is this is because they want a good lunch, a friendly attentive service etc.
So do think about which benefits and services your guests want to provide, deliver their benefits and added value to their guests and to create thus an excellent reputation as a host.
This is also part of the guest loyalty and attract new customers, to give more than is expected of them, that does not mean that you are their guests over to suck up or should even meet in a submissive manner, it is called just what it says - you deliver excellent customer service and service.

Here are some questions you can ask yourself and answer the questions have not necessarily to do with their operations, there are mainly questions interpersonal and private personal space.
But these are no less important as the professional issues.

1. How are my interpersonal relationships be constructed, which meanings are to have relationships for me?

_____

_____

_____

_____

2. With how many people I want to maintain my contact?

___

___

___

___

3. I'd rather be with male or female persons?

___

___

___

4. What and how much time I would spend with my relationships and what to bring me these relationships?

___

___

___

___

5. What role does a partnership in my life?

___

___

___

___

6. What should my / bring a partnership physically and mentally, and will I have a more casual relationship or an intense relationship?

___

___

___

___

7. What are the main features and characteristics should my partner?

___

___

___

___

8. How do I want to feel in the partnership and to what extent should develop my partnership?

_____

_____

_____

_____

9. Should my profession for me just to be earning or self-expression?

_____

_____

_____

10. In which areas of life success is important to me and how should this express?

_____

_____

_____

11. What financial claims I have and what the value of my profession for me and other people?

_____

_____

_____

_____

12. How do I want to feel in the morning when I think about my work and how I want to feel at night when I think about my work during the day?

_____

_____

_____

_____

13. How I want to see me in my body and feel?

_____

_____

_____

_____

14. How will other people react to my body and how I want express myself in my body?

_____

_____

_____

_____

15. What it means to me to be healthy and well?

_____

_____

_____

_____

You will have wondered at some questions, what do these look in a book such as this, is it so?
It makes sense that you are concerned about the issues, because you spend most time with other people and therefore it is important to be clear with what people we are accustomed his daily work.
Also take time while you sit and think about these issues. You must not edit these questions in a passage and beanworten, take the time you need.
I submit to you, however, to the heart, to really deal with these issues.

The Pareto principle converted to the catering

The economist Wilfried Pareto discovered that in all walks of life a ratio from 80 to 20 is observed and so this principle was named after its discoverer Pareto called, the Pareto principle.
As just mentioned, is the Pareto principle, in short the 80/20 rule that a company with 20% of its customers generated 80% of its turnover.
The fact that 80% of total assets are in the hands of 20%.
The fact that 20% of Umfälle cause 80% of the total cost and that 20% of Salesman in a company 80% of the total sales of the sales force generate.
You can use this money anywhere in the world and in all areas watch.

The crux of the whole is now to find out what these 20% do differently than the another 80% and then to reinforce these activities or from another angle formulated to take care of 80% of its work in 20% of the time, do you mean more done in less time.
Today, many leading companies around the world use this principle to their to increase efficiency, to increase their profits and more and more in ever less time to produce.
Well, we are in the restaurant business at home and we can not possibly guests communicate, pass on dear guest, the matter is simple, now you stay as still to yesterday sit no longer 12 bis 13 clock clock on your chair, but standing already back at twenty past zwölf clock back on and go, you just have to eat and drink faster, then we can do that in this time period.
Lunch guests are in a hurry anyway, since we do not need their short lunch time
more unnecessary stress.

So how can we use this principle useful in the restaurant business?

- 80% of the daily sales, and 20% of our best guests.
- 80% of our advertising bring us 20% of new walk-in customers.
- Done 80% of our stress in service and cuisine in 20% of our opening times, the.
 two hours over lunch
- 80% of our beverage sales we do with 20% of our selection of drinks.

The principle is so amazing because you notice it everywhere in operation be (incidentally, also applies to the private sector to) and once you have their actions align it, you can use the opportunities and results with almost mathematical certainty predict.
Then you will first determine where you are wasting money and time and Invest the energy is in proportion to sales and earnings.
When you start using this principle to check its operation and inspect, then you will find where you make money and how to be a bunch of can avoid stress.

What does that mean in real terms?
Consider their menu?

Which meals are going well and bring you the most revenue?
Which never run so to speak, and you just need a bunch of mise en place and place in the cooler and you can then throw away because no one then asks.
Flick their menu together and then all shop keeper out the It only costs money, but bring no revenue.
The same with the drinks, which do not run, so here also, get rid of it.

All this is just dead money and their money to work for you and them sales bring, everything else is just cabbage and turnips that you can do without.
Make room and free yourself from old baggage.

Then check their advertising costs and promotional activities in which actions they are successful and those that were not?
All you have so far brought only money and a low cash flow stress away and step up their advertising where the best and most have reflux.

They will create by these measures not only space, you gain an overview of what's going on and brings them money and what not!

The motto is: less is sometimes more!

And if you're at it, then you declutter also equal to your pantry and their deep freezer.
What stored there for ages, take it out and turn it into a menu or otherwise process it in a way and manner you make of it because of me something and serve it at the bar for happy hour or serve it to their
Complimentary evening as a kind of appetizer.
Be creative, but you drive, and does so consistently with the old crap.

The same that you no longer need with design or machine, perhaps a other host or the hotel owner just such a machine in need of them for ages long standing around.
Photograph the machine or the decorative material and place it into the Internet (free listing or eBay) someone else happy and you deserve it nor money and the machine comes to them out of the way.
So they all have something about you as well as the new owner of their old machine.

Another possibility is, as we in NLP (Neuro Linguistic Programming) say that if a person can do something, it can also be another person the same if they know how something is done.
Translated into practice, this looks as follows:

In every company there are employees the true driving forces are the good one have contact to the customer or guest and a positive mental attitude radiate and convey that simply have fun at what they do.
Questions now their draft horses what they do differently than the average employees as they motivate themselves and what they thought and setting the work and towards other people have.

So find out how these employees, tick their draft horses.

This you can find out best if you are looking for a dialog with them about their to learn thoughts and attitudes.
Once you have figured out what these people make such a to have good relationship to work and to the guests, then write this down and explain this to average employees.
But be careful, you do not say their average employees, I know now Reto or Karin ticks that can so well with the guests, then you are the average employees convey the feeling that I am a whistle.
Say So instead, I have a method or process, as we manage to have a good rapport with our guests, if all of these hold procedure, then everyone can have a good relationship with our guests build and have fun with his work.
Because you just have to have a bit of flair, but that will already are, take heart, because you want to finally their mediocre help colleagues that they will also be better at their job.

Or watch as it will make the best hosts and hoteliers in their area, what or which marketing activities make this, as is their staff trained, what their menu from.
Go quiet time to their competitors in its operation and talk to him of.
They are (as I know from personal experience) to see that other people are more than willing to help them, but you'll have to ask them clearly and say what you want from other people, whether its advice or a good tip etc.
Align and are always based on the best staff and best to bring businesses in their area to learn what make this so they are so successful.
If you have found in conversations with their best employees what these do differently, then set this.
The same applies to other successful companies, which make this different from the masses and then take over their successful strategies.

As I said, if you know how successful people do something and you then know how these people or businesses do this and then the apply the same winning strategies, then you will also have similar or even achieve even better results.
This has nothing to do with espionage, you simply want to find out how you can still can be successful and to simply look at the successful people in the Industry on the fingers, that's all ☺

The Pareto principle summarized again:

Find out which introduce dishes with 20% effort 80% yield and you push this, everything else Unnecessary tilt of the map.
- Find out what drinks to bring the most revenue and little cost in purchasing, so their source of revenue and think about how you can accelerate.
- Create order and air in their warehouse which machines you have is no longer being used and only take them off course, photograph them and make their offer then the internet, someone others will be glad to be able to buy them their machine.

- Which employees are their draft horses, find out how they work and what attitude they have and then put this in their entire operation around so that also enables the mediocre employees are have to improve and enjoy their work.
- Operate quietly spy something in their prime competitors by find out what these do better than others and consider then how you can apply this knowledge to their business.
- *In general, what you should be less and what you should do more!*
- What activities lead to results that far exceed the time and energy beyond that you need to invest in it, where is the biggest benefit and to achieve sales in the least time.

Copy successful business models on their operation and their guests, find out what the most successful make in the relevant sector and most importantly, how they do it. Find out what and how the best people to work in their operations so the other employees can copy and take over their attitude to similar or the same to get good results and outcomes.

Ask the question asked, the Steve Jobs (deceased chief of Apple) has:
"If today were the last day of my life, would I do what I 'm going to do today? "

If you can answer yes to this question and more often, then you are on a good way and if not, then you're wondering what I would need in my change lives, so the answer to these questions is yes?

Personal notes and implementation points:

1. _____

   _____

   _____

2. _____

   _____

   _____

   _____

3. _____

   _____

   _____

   _____

4. _____

   _____

   _____

   _____

5. _____

   _____

   _____

From imitators and other evildoers

Always be yourself and realize their own ideas and concepts, As I have described them in the previous chapter, you should be from the best always cut a slice in the industry and see how and what they do so that they are successful.
But you should not be a cheap copy of another, unless you work for a franchise business where required of them that you their products and logos, because you are contractually obliged and bound to it.

Do you know the definition of insanity?
„If you do always the same, while hoping other results are coming! »

Thus, if a company must make its doors forever tight, because the sales and guests are becoming more and more fell, then the new owner should not make the mistake of using the same methods and staff there again to establish where its predecessor left off.
Why should not employees be adopted?
Because - People are creatures of habit - and like to do something like it have always done it, because they know this way and they are familiar with.
I once had an operation over which went into bankruptcy and thus the Could continue operating without interruption, in short I have the entire acquired workforce, because I could not carry alone the whole store.
Many of the long-established staff, I had to resign then because they simply to firmly drive were on the old farm structures, even before we have the so-and made so no that will not do what we have never done so, etc.
I made this clear to people then that sooner now times over and that today Today, and I can not continue in the same old rut as before and wants.

And the other reason is:
These people spreading negative energy with their attitude and sayings and are designed to operate over a brake as a real profit and benefit.
That may at first sound harsh, but it is unfortunately the case, and therefore you need to draw a line and the past.

You and I can not afford to play the welfare office, you have neither the time nor the energy to do, to deal with people who only ever want to take and give nothing in return.
This can make as I said at the office such people, but not in their operation.
Evildoers and people who are interested not really with them together to bring the operation forward, neither use them nor their guests and you should therefore be separated from such people.
I know that a dismissal is never a pleasant thing, and I have also always done hard time, but you must act in the interests of their company and can it simply not afford such people and effort be feeding and to not only overcome from a social vein out to may terminate this.

There is another category of offenders in their own ranks encountered before and which you should beware!
Friends and good acquaintances.

If you have a business, it is often the case that friends to them come to want to work with them!
I and other business owners have in this respect, unfortunately, poor had experiences that some of the friends work very good use and other their status (because you're friends) and you have a hard time with such people like to talk with another employee, true to the motto: how say I my child.
And often waits and you look for too long, until one finally falls to action and these people (friends) have to say, watch dear ... so it does not go and we must part again.
Therefore applies here weigh very carefully what friends and acquaintances in want to employ their operation or not!
Tell them her belly no, then you communicate this friendly but determined because, here too, you are not for the welfare of other people responsible and you are also not required to give someone who is her boyfriend calls to stop.

Ask your friend or acquaintance peaceful, why he or she is working for them want and why you should hire him (just because they are friends and by you), what you should arrange his view, adjust their acquaintances.
I know with friends you do not speak otherwise in that tone, but believe me I also speak from experience here and I know that you a lot of trouble can barter for when you set the Known more harm than good cause.
In this way, you and your operation is helped in any way, the opposite is the case, screwed up is quickly built something and established, however, takes longer and is a difficult process.
Make the Opposite quiet clear that you are friends indeed, but that this need not necessarily be glad that you set this person must, because that person has just become unemployed and thinks, oh the Hans Meier is a nice guy, because I can not go to work and doing a quiet ball slide, but because we've known each other for so long!
I know entrepreneurs who have fallen, to any "friends" and thereby have had bad experiences.
This does not mean that you set basically no friends and acquaintances should I just say, you pay very careful when you set and what motives that person moves to work with them.
Will one, because that is a good friend and a nice guy just a quiet Ball moves, then he can do that, but not in their operation and their costs.

So be careful when "good friends" knock on them and to seek a job, it can go well but also not.
It is important that you make clear at the outset how things are going in their operation and what you expect and (very important) even friends for you work according to the same rules to behave as everyone else and that you make because employees no exception.

You are no one owe anything and just because "a good friend" you know, you are still far from being obliged to offer this for a job.

Distancing yourself from people you do want proof that you would need.
Do you have anything that is.

If you use clear words (as I've done it after I've had bad experiences), it may also happen that it is their then change your mind acquaintances and friends differently and then but not with them want to work.
Why do these people have it then sets suddenly different, can they not matter in the end, it shows them only then that after you clear words to Have brought the debate or friends this is not quite fit has or ought to have, and they have played in the back of the head with the idea in to push them pretty cushy.
I disagree gladly say it again, you are not for life and the job of their friends and acquaintances responsible, any more than this for their operation and their sales are responsible.
So you do not have to play the welfare office for other people.
Believe me, so you can save yourself a lot of trouble and as a successful Restaurateur, you can all do, interested and motivated employees new Ideas, but certainly not the anger can be avoided right from the beginning.

So beware of evildoers and copy anybody, get out of other ideas and suggestions and then make their own things, because nothing liable to the stuffiness of the lack of creativity more than a bad imitation copy.

<u>Copy successful ideas and concepts, but turn it into their own thing and not a cheap copy, their guests, it will not buy them, only if They have their own identity and concept, you appear credible.</u>

Again, as in chapter for which you want to be known, you will find their own way and their own personal peculiarity what you and your operation of all other differs.
This is a process that is not completed overnight and it needs creativity and a certain amount of imagination.
More I betray them in the next chapter.

Make your own thing with your own ideas and is good.

Personal notes and implementation points.

1. _____

   _____

   _____

2. _____

   _____

   _____

3. _____

   _____

   _____

4. _____

   _____

   _____

5. _____

   _____

   _____

The necessary imagination

If you can imagine it in your mind and thoughts, then you can create it!

What distinguishes a Bill Gates, Steve Jobs or Donald Trump of other people?
It's who their imagination by a vision of these men in their minds and the considerations to make these visions into reality and as long as further make until they have realized.
Another word for imagination is auto-suggestion and comes from the Latin and means as much as: the ability to influence yourself or the evocation of ideas without external cause by self-influence.

Well, you do not like Donald Trump to build a real estate empire, or to want to try to revolutionize the IT sector, but what you absolutely need for their professional success, a very clear picture of what you have and want to achieve.

I will now explain why this is so important to them!
From science and quantum physics is well known that our Thoughts from energy exist and the whole world is an energy field, ranging from the smallest molecules and atoms.
I'm at this point not elaborate on that subject (not that it would be uninteresting, quite the contrary, but alone would report on an already complete book and you want to yes learn about guest loyalty, not true) but simply refer to a fact that already many well-known personalities from politics Knew culture and economy from the past to the future and always know yet.
Thoughts have the ability to materialize!
A severe sentence is not it, so I'm repeating it here again at this point so you can see that this is no typo:
Thoughts have the ability to materialize!
We're not talking about pseudo-scientific mumbo-jumbo or a surreal wishy washy sauce, but rather of facts readers.

Our imagination is like having a navigation device, enter the coordinates where you want to go and follow the directions.
With the imagination, it is similar, you create and get a clear Idea of what you want to clear images of the desired paint and hold it firmly.
Would they ever noticed that you have a wish, always have thought back to the desired option and then one day (for whatever ever reason) you got exactly what you wanted.
And then you thought, wow - what a coincidence or luck, I always wanted to already have is something like this ever happened to them?
I am sure that you have experienced such a situation ever!
And I admit to note, paint in their mental images of it from what you want to achieve and where you want to be, of all that you make clear Ideas.

You it does not come to mind, just something in their device typing and then just start driving times, use your navigation device to in order to get the quickest route from A to B.

From Bill Gates to know now that he had a clear idea how the world should be linked once, he had Internet Explorer for a long time in his head, and he knew that you will somehow manage this, his vision to realize.
And you and I know, he has found a way.

You need to remember a set, I have also noticed him and see today much with different eyes:

"If you can create something in your mind, then you can created it in the real world! "

You need to yet another fact to be aware of!
All her clothes you wear, the car to go, the kitchen or the Combi steamers you have to stand at in operation, all that is first in the Been thoughts of a person before the into tangible reality and thus dresses van or combi steamer was.
Such people are called designer or kitchen fitter.
Everything in life is always created twice, first in thought and then in the Reality that you make for yourself the test if you do not believe me.
If you create a 5 course meal, then get first thoughts as these five courses will look like in detail, while you already get a first idea of how the courts should taste and how they served should be to deliver a beautiful picture on the plate.
So you have first given some thought and you've also had some Ideas in my head as what might fit together and then have it made to convert these ideas into visible and edible dishes.

This is the small but important secrets which you should be aware of maybe you have been doing certain things unconsciously or have thought that anything in the way could be sure, but you had never a proof that it is so.
You now have the proof, black on white.

For these reasons, you should their inner navigation system (your Imagination) to use things in their minds imagine how They want to see their operation in the future.
I do this way every day, I ask myself before my company as in two to three shall be four years, as it presents itself to the public as I lectures speeches and think, books signiere etc.
And, as I said have all the great visionaries like Bill Gates and Steve Jobs exactly this ingredient, use your imagination to around to see what they are in the future want to see, namely how their products (Windows Apple) of millions or even billions of people are used every day.

Whether, consciously or unconsciously, all men have done the great things and have advanced mankind knew about the power of our imagination.
Everything is created twice, first in our thoughts and with our hands and by our actions.

If the Windows operating system on every day by millions of people used all over the world, and whether I use at the moment the Windows Word where I'm just going to write the rough draft of this book.

Do you have an IPhone, IPad or IMac?
You see, just like you use millions or even billions of other people in the world at this moment is a product of Windows or Apple or both together.
Ueli Pragger also had a vision when he made his first Mövenpick restaurant opened, the idea was new and of the catering and competitors, he was ridiculed, but history teaches us a lesson once again, Mövenpick was and is still today a global player.
Or think of Mc Donalds, its founder Richard and Maurice performed a new and more rational way of making a hamburger and put it on self-service.
What is Mc Donalds today, the fastest growing fast food chain worldwide. and by the way, who was one of the two brothers at that time, in 1940 already 55 years old, but that has not prevented him from simply time to step on the gas and its Implement vision.

Or the department store chain Woolworths is also due to the imagination and vision of its founder created.
All the people I have them listed here, all of which once had a vision and idea and you have their idea painted really big in her thoughts and dreams.
The past and the present is so full of examples of men and to take advantage of women who have understood it their imagination for their own purposes and use.
Stood behind all these companies and achievements, and there are always people with a vision, with a big vision and these men and women were and are convinced of your vision.

So Catch quiet again to dream, other entrepreneurs and gastronomy experts have done it before them and what is the outcome, the you know yourself.
So keep your imagination alive and believe in their idea and tell yourself simply times out loud:

YES WHY NOT!
WHY SHOULD NOT FOLD, OTHERS HAVE IT ALSO
DONE, SO WHY SHOULD I DO NOT EVEN THE CAN!

Yes, why not indeed?
At best you are faced with a mirror and ask yourself this questions above, why not??
The problem with most people is not that they have no desires or goals have, they do not believe in yourself!
And if someone does not believe in themselves, then it becomes difficult another to convince person because only if a person believes in himself and of their idea is firmly convinced, then she has this magical aura around of other people is perceived as contagious and pulsating.
And it is this contagious conviction of the initiators can also be other people believe in the feasibility of the idea or project.

If you have the vision in your imagination the best restaurant or hotel to be in the whole region, if you know and have found out what you want to be known to the public, then submit their imagination with these thoughts and hold them, their vision is always upright.

Then you will realize that to change things in their favor start, maybe not immediately, but things are starting to be in the desired direction to move, because you start to use their focus targeted.
Remember what is important to them and where you want, do not think more started a bunch of confused thoughts, no, you have the whole day to ignite their mental Turbo and every day you go to it.
People and situations will encounter them and suddenly you realize, and you will be surprised and amazed, because all that (these people and situations and opportunities) bring further progress towards your goal.
It's almost a little magical as it anmutet itself, but have in fact just begun to make their imagination advantage and thus also the power of their thoughts and their subconscious.
These are powerful allies and if you own only times the power of their have recognized thought, then you are sure to always targeted to thinking.

Anyone can achieve amazing success when it the deepest layers of his
Psyche can work specifically for themselves.

By a person, no matter whether it is for negative or positive thoughts ideas or emotions are consciously designed, this person may be dominate consciousness and learn to think what he wants to think.
Through our thinking we humans have the ability to our imagination or even deliberately to influence autosuggestion and control.
At any moment, even in the ereignislosesten, flow thoughts and feelings one on our subconscious and our psyche and they affect us often subtle manner, it is not even aware of the people.

He feels good or bad, evil spirits or elated and he do not know why or why, he thinks, is probably just a freak of nature.
But exactly this nature has provided us with our mental and physical abilities as well as our free will, given the opportunities in a decisive way to determine what information sent to our subconscious not to be and what.
In other words, you have it in hand so what thoughts and feelings You want, how you want to feel and what thoughts you Want to pay attention to and what not.
However, many people of this control function are not aware of and access therefore not attributed, because they so far no one has said that they their can control and steer thoughts and feelings.

To me it is important that you know about about dear reader and if you are ask at the moment, which has to do with the whole guest loyalty, then you will realize that everything is a question of their thoughts.

Because of the professional and personal success and well-being has everything with our do attitude and our beliefs, perhaps in many unconscious and they know, though intuitively what is right and what wrong
And also, has a bit of knowledge about the functioning of our thinking never hurt anyone, so I have dedicated to them also this chapter because I am of the opinion that it is important.

Success or failure arises in our thinking and feeling, it is not the competitors or the economy, they may have a certain influence even no question, but the decisive factor is how and what we think for themselves.
If you are convinced that their operation no green branch come, come on no green branch, no matter what you do or do not make, make with their mental attitude that everything do (albeit unconsciously) that you will not succeed.
Then you can say to yourself, I've just knew that something which is never!
And then you have the confirmation of the self-fulfilling prophecy.

Success or failure will be decided between our two ears in our thinking.

It is also important that you learn about the workings of our thinking learn, and you will realize that you have very well have something for your well-being and can contribute to your success.
And if they are aware of this, you further recognize that it in hand and be able to control the success and learn to control their thoughts consciously to achieve confident results.
And that's why this issue should also be in a book like this.

I want to give you an example from my life:
I am often asked by people how I did this or that?
Then I have to tell these people I do not know either, I just had my goal in mind and then have taken steps in the direction of my goal, while people and circumstances I have encountered who helped me with this or have support on my way.
Retrospectively, I can just say I had my goal in mind and I have leave me that I reach my goal, sometimes I knew in each moment and not know how I should do this, but I was just the firm conviction that I at the right time the right incentives or promptings will receive.
And so it was.

Initially, I wanted to spread my knowledge and therefore sought for a newspaper in Internet, it did not work right away and after a few attempts, I came across Happy Times and my idea was well suited in its concept.
Today I write for several years a weekly column each saturday morning appears, and thousands of readers and readers in german-speaking countries is read.
From these weekly articles out then the book series was concluded with frustration of it to this day already four volumes as well as an anthology are working together with book on Amazon to buy.
As a Kindle reader, or in paperback.

And soon there will be an online course for the book series, with videos and documents for daily use, with the goal of leading a more fulfilling life.

This course will be available on the online platform Diplomero.
So you see, was only just the idea to spread my knowledge there and it took a moment until I'm finally become aware of Happy Times.
I was at the right time at the right place now, some think of the readers, yes but partly also because I had a clear idea of what I wanted.
And because of what I wanted, I focused also according to I found what I was looking for and needed.
The rest is history.

Or another example from practice that occurs determines them known!
You have certainly already for a car brand and a particular model this brand is interested.
What happened after that?
You saw on the road again this car brand and this model for that you care!
Question - there were now more cars of this brand and this model than before?
Answer - no, it falls to them now only aware of because your focus exactly on this model from this manufacturer direct.
The same is true for expectant mothers, pregnant women, there are now more than before, NO, they have focused only on themselves because they are pregnant.
And therefore fall forward to the things to which our attention to our focus have directed.

When we or the hotel owner should focus their attention to their guests and their wishes and have needs and always ask the question, how can I get my offer guests an even better service?
As you explore the needs and desires of their guests better and find out about it I tell them in the next chapter.

But first, I hope that you have received a couple of instructive information as our thinking works and what it does to the imagination about and how You can use for their professional and personal success of these targeted.
And again, once again, practice makes perfect, if you're starting not achieve the same desired results, that does not mean that you therefore have failed, you should just go ahead persistent.
The Success will come down sooner or later inevitably, stay true to its course and use their imagination every day of the operation their dreams.
So once again, let's go dear reader ☺

Personal notes and implementation points

1. _____

_____

_____

2. _____

_____

_____

3. _____

_____

_____

4. _____

_____

_____

5. _____

_____

_____

Deliver what is desired!

You have great ideas and have implemented this and then you wonder why none of the guests really make friends with their new idea and concept can?
Now, something you should also note in this regard!
If you find something good and great, then does that not long that your guests also this great and good find.

The best way to find out if something arrives at their guests or not, is that you do a survey of their guests and passers-by on the road.
Proceed methodically with the aim of a good information about it get what people want, because there are their guests and potential guests you want to address to find out what Wüschen this.

Do you want to know how their guests will adore the interior or what better could be, then make out a survey?
Do you want to know what food their guests want to eat with them, or whether there are drinks after which there is a demand, then make a survey.
Because ... you can have a great idea but that does not necessarily mean because you find something great that your guests find their ideas also great, so you can find the Needs of their guests the best way out that you can order these their ask opinion.
And you know already from the previous chapters that people appreciate it when they are asked for their opinion, because that they convey to the other person, you are important and I'm interested in your opinion for me.

And thus you have the certainty that deliver what their customers want and what she is willing to pay for it, because you can control their surveys so that you end up with an accurate idea of what their guests want.

Ask your guests and here are a few examples of what you're their guest or can ask people on the street!
Adjust so that you are tailored to your operation, the questions together.

- What do you miss in our company?
- What you will find is good and what you will find less good?
- Would you appreciate it if we place a menu of three menus newly offer choice, if so, one of the menus there should be vegetarian or what kind of menu you would welcome?
- What do you think that is open on Sundays and at what times?
- What do you like about our company and what you love about our employees special?

Ask specific questions of what and how, so that people come to think and do not questions that can be answered with a simple yes or no.

When you take on the road with pedestrians, a survey because you want to find out what kind of food and the people operating would welcome, then you could ask questions of the following type!

- What kind of restaurant you would welcome in (name of town) and why?
- What is missing gastronomic their opinion, in (name of town)?
- What should a new restaurant / hotel for you so that you have there would come regularly?
- How often do you eat out and how much do you spend on average per visit from the restaurant?
- Do you have a favorite restaurant and why is (operation name) her favorite restaurant?

These questions should serve as their support and encouragement, it is important that you Questions of how and why formulate, so that people really have to think why this why they like something or some things are important.

It is precisely these points you want to find out yes, that is what people or say the masses want and why it's important that you at least two hundred people on the street surveys.

The more completed surveys, the better, because that you have an even better picture of what wants the masses.

If you do not want to make even the polls, organize someone makes for the survey, this may be something the young people themselves Want to earn pocket money or seniors, you will always find someone who interviewed other people and then listed their answers to the survey sheets.

But even here you should make sure that you reliable people for the job who can also approach the people and also the answers legibly note on the survey sheets.

Because it does not make sense two - to have three hundred completed questionnaires the however, you can not read because they are written so illegible.

Then take all the completed questionnaires together and they are from for example, when asked whether they would welcome it if sunday would be open and have at what times, more than 150 people responded with yes and have given as opening times from bis neun clock achtzehn clock to answer, then is an indication that people welcome it if it to sundays restaurants can range from morning to evening eighteen clock.

For it may be that in the whole area not a single restaurant is open on Sundays and therefore the population is a need that they have the have opportunity to go to a restaurant on sunday.

Or when asked what gastronomic missing, many answers have the content that place in a restaurant missing with good hearty meals at reasonable prices, then you know that the masses want to eat home-style cooking on the road and this at a reasonable price.

So no Schicki Miki but good and cheap.

Now that you know what people want from the road, then you should have a create flyers and distribute these throughout the village and or even into the neighboring communities.
For what it uses when you now know what is needed and no is made aware that you are offering exactly that.

A flyer could include the following text:

Dear residents and residents

***You have chosen and the choice fell with a triumphant majority on the candidates good and cheap from the restaurant (operation name)
Our newly nominated candidates Good and cheap are now over seven
Days a week in the evenings from (opening times of food)
found our home and are happy you revered residents and
To be able to offer a resident of (community) adhere to a gourmet evening.***

Good candidate: Pork steak with rosti potato croquettes and vegetables $ / £ 17

Candidate Cheap: vegetables with fried egg and croutons $ / £ 9

The election winner Good and cheap and the entire team from the hotel / Restaurant (operation name) looking forward to your visit.

For this purpose, you can also add a funny picture, because the Flyers to a quiet bit funny and saucy come because this loosens up and lets the operating appear in a positive light.
And also applies here, go new and creative ways of attracting visitors and stand out from the gray crowd, this was in the guest extraction or of advertising.

Let their creative potential run wild and you are looking forward to a huge response, the witty and striking their advertising, the more guests and new customers you will attract and tighten.
However, as already mentioned, you focus their efforts on the needs and concerns from their guests, because these are the ones which are coming into their operations and them to bring in sales.
You may like to have an idea, but clarify beforehand on whether this is also a Is need of their guests, and if so, set the Planned order and deliver you want what.

Personal notes and implementation points:

1. _____

_____

_____

2. _____

_____

_____

3. _____

_____

_____

4. _____

_____

_____

5. _____

_____

_____

What we can learn from Steve Jobs

Steve Jobs, the co-founder of Apple who passed away a few years ago always glided still considered one of the most innovative entrepreneurs in economic history.
2010 elected the American newspaper Fortune Steve Jobs Entrepreneur of the Decade, and Thomas Friedman, the well-known columnist for the New York Times wrote in an article that America is more "jobs" needs and wanted to express that it is necessary to promote innovation and creativity.
Exactly this innovation and creativity is to flourish a company and if more companies are creative and innovative, helps the community to come to the recession.

In his book "The Innovation Secrets of Steve Jobs", the author describes Mc Graw - Hill, 2010, the seven main principles on which the breakthrough success based Apple.
These principles are fundamental principles according to which each of them followed attain success in his business and since this book it is, success have and to the reader to show ways how it can be successful, I have given you these seven principles listed here.

You remember the chapter on the Pareto principle, find out what other successful people and companies make, copy the behavior and strategies for their own business and you will be like achieve results.
Copy the strategies but you are not a cheap copy of your model and they reserve the question in their own identity and originality.

So let's now take a look behind the motives and motivation of a Steve Jobs throw, have how and what thought processes led this man to make a company like Apple so successful worldwide.

Lets take a look inside, right?

1. Principle: DO THE WHAT YOU LOVE.

In 2005, Steve Jobs told the Stanford course completion University of the secret of his success lies in having the courage of his heart and intuition to follow.
In his experience, everyone knew already inside, what he really wants.
Steve Jobs has always followed his heart throughout his career.
His own opinion, it is precisely this suffering - Community, the the makes significant difference.
It's hard to develop new and creative ideas that a society can advance, if you are not really excited for it.

Steve Jobs once said, it would be better as a waitress or the like work until you find something for which you can really inspire, "I am convinced that what successful companies from unsuccessful differs, about half represents pure perseverance. If you do not can muster passion for something, you'll never reach your goal. you 'll give up"

However, as you find your passion?
Passion manifests itself mainly in ideas, one can no more rest.
They are the hopes, dreams and possibilities, of which the own thoughts are met.
Follow this enthusiasm despite all the skeptics and naysayers who themselves not muster the courage to pursue her own dreams.

2. Principle: LEAVE FOOTPRINTS IN THE UNIVERSE.

Steve Jobs was enthusiastic staff who shared his vision and helped him convert his ideas into global innovation.
He never underestimate how important it is to have a clear vision for a brand advance.

1976 was inspired by Steve Wozniak Jobs idea of having a computer for to develop everyday use.
Wozniak was the engineering genius behind Apple 1 and Apple 2, but it was Jobs Vision Wozniak to brought in to build a computer for his skills bring in the masses.
Jobs vision was intoxicating because it contained four components that all inspiring visions have in common: they were first bold 2 targeted 3 concise and 4th consistently communicated.

1979 Jobs visited the Xerox Research Division in Palo Alto California.
He saw there a new technology that allows users based colorful graphic symbols could interact on the screen with the computer rather than the need to enter complex line commands.

This was called "graphical user interface".
At this moment Jobs knew that this technologist would enable him to realize his vision of a computer for everyone in the act.
Back in his office, Steve Jobs taught his team out of the computer to develop who was ultimately known as Macintosh and forever the way changed how we communicate with computers.

Steve Jobs later said that Xerox would dominate the computer industry can.
But the goal of Xerox would have consisted only of a new copier to bring to the market.

3. Principle: BRING YOUR BRAIN IN FULL SWING

Creativity for innovative ideas.
For Steve Jobs meant creativity, to connect things together.
He believed that a breadth of experience and understanding of the people extended.
A broad understanding can lead to innovations and breakthroughs that other missed.

Breakthrough innovation is based on creativity and creativity requires a different way of thinking - about the way how to think.
Scientists who study the human brain, have discovered that Innovators actually think differently, but they use a technique on the we all have: they draw from diverse experiences and link them.

This reminds me of the story of the name Apple.
The idea was in the literal sense of a tree.
Steve Jobs came back from visiting a commune in Oregon, which is on the site of an apple orchard was, Wozniak, Jobs co-founder and friend, took him from the airport.
On the way home, Jobs said that he have a name for the company found was: Apple.
Wozniak said that they would have a tech-sounding name can use, but their vision was indeed the fact, computers for the masses to make accessible.
The name Apple fit there quite well.

Jobs developed new ideas, because he did all his days new and not explored interrelated things and doing a variety of experiences made.
Jobs set the did not come from the computer industry employees.
He studied at a college, the art of calligraphy (calligraphy), meditated in an Indian ashram, analyzed the details of a Mercedes Benz model and European washing machines and dryers to product ideas to designing.

In addition, he analyzed the development of the service model of Apple stores, the hotel chain "The Four Seasons".
By repeatedly appropriated new experiences, he freed himself from the shackles of past experiences.

4. Principle: SELLING DREAMS, NOT PRODUCTS

Steve Jobs has never rely on focus groups, "It is a fact that the most customers can not really tell what a new product should be able to " Analyst Rob Enderle said the tech.

Apple customers can be happy that Steve Jobs is not the Focus Groups had supported.
Had he done so, it would be the iPod, iTunes, the iPhone, the iPad and the Apple Stores may not even exist.
He did not need focus groups because he understood his customers themselves very well.
When Jobs returned in 1997 after 12 years of absence to Apple, was the companies face an uncertain future.
Jobs ended his presentation that year at Macworld in Boston with an observation that was decisive for the resurgence of Apple: "I am believes you have to think differently to buy an Apple computer. I believe that the people who buy an Apple computer in fact different „thinking"
They are the creative spirits in the world.

These are not people who are just out of it, a job to do, these are people who want to change the world.
And they want to change the world for the latest best tools they can get.
We provide exactly these tools for such people here ... it is often said that they are crazy, but we see in this madness something brilliant. "

"This, however, does not mean that you never listen to its customers and by should ask feedback. Apple always does this. But the sweeping success of Apple was based primarily on the innovative ideas of Jobs and his team.
When asked why Apple integrates no focus groups, Jobs responded: "We find out for yourself what direction we want to pursue, you can customers not just ask, What is to come next? "
There is a great quote from Henry Ford, he said, "If my customers would have asked according to their wishes, they would have demanded a faster horse. "

Nobody is interested in your business or your products.
People are busy with their own things, their dreams and goals.
Steve Jobs was able to win people over by helping them meet their goals to reach.

5. Principle: SAY NO TO A THOUSAND THINGS.

Steve Jobs once said that the secret of innovation is to a thousand things to say no.
In other words, Jobs was as proud of what Apple had never realized, as to what Apple eventually pursued.
He felt committed to a simple clean design.
This philosophy has enabled Apple to continuously offer products that Enthusiastic customers by their elegance and simplicity.

In October 2008, Apple introduced its next-generation MacBook laptop.
Jobs invited to Apple's design guru Jonathan Ive live a on the stage the new to explain the manufacturing process for mobile computing, which allowed Apple to produce lighter and at the same time more stable notebooks.
Ive told the audience that Apple's new unibody aluminum 60 percent of the main components made superfluous.
By eliminating these parts of the computer will naturally thinner and easier.
Contrary to expectations, the new laptop is thereby also curing and more robust.
Ive said, "We are 100 percent focused on simple and clear solutions to develop because as physical beings we appreciate the clarity and transparency. "

Customers want simplicity.
And simplicity requires that you eliminate things that users experience the confront - be it in product design, in the websites navigation, in marketing in advertising materials or presentation slides.

6. Principle: CREATE UNFORGETTABLE, CRAZY EXPERIENCES

Steve Jobs brought the Apple Store to the gold standard in customer service.
The Apple Store is now the world's best retail company.
It generates more revenue per area than most other comparable brands and provides simple innovations that can take over for each company, build up to more intense and more personal customer relationships.
For example, there are no cashiers in an Apple store, there are experts and consultants and even geniuses, but no cashiers.
According jobs people do not want to simply buy a computer more: "You want to know what they can do with it, and that's what we show them. "

Apple created an innovative shopping experience by a company to model adopted, which is known for its excellent customer service, the hotel chain Four Seasons.

According to Ron Johnson, Senior Vice President of Retail Operations at Apple, would Apple Stores the buyer does not thereby attract by cartons out - and are shuffled, but by "enriching life."
Apple offers a customer experience like at the front desk of an elegant hotel.
The lesson is that way from the crate slide image.
Jobs and Apple want to "enrich life" instead and this principle was to a great success.

7. Principle: A DOMINANT THE MESSAGE

You can use the most innovative idea in the world have, but if you can not make it
To get people excited about this idea, it does not matter.
For every idea that leads to a successful innovation, there are thousands of Ideas that have not gained a foothold because the people behind these ideas are not in were able to tell a compelling story.

Steve Jobs is considered one of the greatest storytellers of the business world, his presentations were informative, instructive and entertaining.
His extraordinary presentations made him a leading figure and a great communicator. He knew that Apple was assessed in a high mass then, as he managed to convey the company's mission credible.
The big difference between extraordinary communicators and the average leader is that people like about their jobs Presentations complemented their message.
The speaker is a storyteller, the presentation serves as background to the history.

So dear reader, now you have an insight into the mindset of the man received was world-renowned for its innovative ideas, a man with a clear vision of where he wanted to lead Apple.
And as you have read, understood how Steve Jobs as no other people to help meet their goals.
The more people you help and help that these goals and their Wishes to achieve, the more successful and prosperous you too will be.

What is your vision and message for your customers and employees?

Personal notes and implementation points:

1. _____

_____

_____

2. _____

_____

_____

3. _____

_____

_____

4. _____

_____

_____

5. _____

_____

_____

People have desires and needs!

People have needs and desires, and they go there or to the people or organizations where they know that they and their wishes get needs met.
If you have an accident with your car, then you also hope that the breakdown service will help you to fix the glitch and you will can continue.

In Internet Marketing there is an expression, infusiones marketing and means as much as, its potential customers step by step information to type which have the purpose to create a need and a desire in him; yes I want and what I need.
Even in the field of advertising and marketing has in the past years, done a lot, but unfortunately, so many restaurateurs have not yet realized that they 0815 with advertising no one from the bush, resp. from can lure her living room in their operation.

Make time for yourself a following test?
Take on TV or in magazines or newspapers on the advertising?
What are you not talking to and what which you will be remembered and which you have already forgotten again after the newspaper aside or turn off the TV?

I'm sure (without knowing you personally) that the one advertising has addressed that have your feelings and emotions addressed, also has triggered a reaction inside of you.
The folks at Mercedes Benz are there very clever way and you should at times their advertising, pay attention:
There, you is not just a nice new car shown that through the area leads and to appear a few specifications.
No, you see a driver or a pair in the car sits and relaxes the driver has a smile on his lips, you can also see the bad out weather conditions are still so that the driver has no problem, he knows that he in his Mercedes Benz thanks to the technology and innovation in all weather conditions safely is underway and will achieve its objective.

Here, then, values and desires are like safety, comfort and driving pleasure conveys all the things wants a motorist to him a good and safe convey feeling.
And exactly this feeling of wanting the advertisers of Mercedes and its customers convey Dear customer, no matter what the weather is coming, our car you healed in all weather conditions at the destination, you can rely on us and your ride enjoy.
Interesting data such as fuel consumption or exhaust maintenance or alloy wheels but the potential new customers less, he wants safety and driving pleasure.

The following two sentences, you should remember, because they are important.

Because the feeling of security is a basic human need.

Remember, you need your future guests on an emotional level pick up.

As I said, people have wants and needs and the better you know the wishes and needs of their customers, the better your business will walk and guests will you be breaking down the booth, because you at your get what you want and give you the feeling you get with me what you wish dear guest.

The following sentence you should remember also, because this is also important.

Then the price is a lot, since it's always about the result and nothing else.

As a restaurateur, you must also start in advertising to rethink exactly for the reason previously liked the 0815 advertising still work, but today no more.
Because the people who daily einprasselt by the flood of information on them, are blunted, every week flutter any brochures in the mailbox, in the Supermarket pushes them the cashier even a note in the hand with the note that this is a new lottery etc.
And all this advertising is the same as the other, everything is what will change the logo and
the company and its products, but the principle and the message is the same; buy with me dear customer!
But why should I at the company X buy when I the same product or a can also buy similar at the company Z?

The point of this type of advertising, it is not aimed at the product but on the need or desire of the customer, so you will hardly read and lands to paper.

Make it so different now!
A classic example that I see over and over again: Serve Every Friday evening we in our restaurant fondue chinoise a discretion with a glass Champagne as an aperitif for only £ / $ 24
Ok, well and good, but why I have no real, or shall we say good reason to go there, as a fondue I can also at an other place order!
So why expect this host that I come to him only because of his fondue he offers every Friday night, ah yes, a glass of champagne is still in the price included, well, but that's why I still have no particular reason to go to this restaurant!
Do you understand what I'm prefer to readers?

In this above example (as it is still far too often practiced) gives me the Host or the hotel owner, who is hoping to talk to me, no apparent reason why should I go to him what he has what another does not?
He is one of many and creates in me I do not really need the inner, II must now necessarily indicate otherwise I missing something.

I am still just as good if I place this operation in a different operation going.
In this way, way too much money is useless thrown out the window and the
Restaurateur of this display switched, maybe even several times in a combi offer the local newspaper wonders then why the reaction to his display has generated such a low response!

The text was still beautiful and the photo but also somehow managed and moreover, the whole thing was still expensive pork.
Pigs expensive listings are far from being a guarantee for new guests and more sales!

You need to address the emotional state of your target audience with your advertising and awaken an inner need and desire by the customer, an internal reaction cause, he must have the desire to get what you offer him have, the faster the better.
Just like the guys from Mercedes, who knows the ropes and are the aware that you can respond and pick up his customers on an emotional level needs.
Do as Steve Jobs and try to give the people what they want and desire.

For example, if you have a hotel and want to appeal to couples who could then to create a text by the following contents:
"Do you remember the time when you were newly in love, the electrifying feeling the butterflies in my stomach and how the whole world has smiled upon you. "
In the morning, wake up next to his treasure and with his smile and a gentle kiss to be awakened - you feel completely happy and satisfied.
Enjoy this wonderful feeling again together with your partner and let yourself be enchanted, you will feel fresh in love again.
With us you can expect after your arrival a fragrant foam tape with rose oil and a bottle of chilled champagne in your cozy comfortable rooms.
Then it goes for a walk in beautiful landscape where another Surprise waiting for you and your partner.
In the evening, a dreamy candlelight dinner runs to stay where you are and your partner all to yourself have time to forget about everyday life.
Before retiring to your cozy comfortable room awaits you Let nightcap, put together especially for you Both of our home, Surprise yourself and enjoy beautiful romantic days in our home - you deserve it.

Well how this reads?
Definitely more enjoyable than as a dry unimaginative advertising text outdated anyway no one really reads.

The whole text has come a bit long, but it is also more to me the idea and the incentive to transfer a desire and need with your Message, yes I will meet with my partner a beautiful Experience the weekend, only for both of us time for cuddles and sensual moments.
If you do not want texts themselves, so let's texts but be sure to that the message you want to send, the recipient receives your message is to awaken emotions and to generate a pulse of desire.

Throughout the text you pack more into the appropriate font and flourishes a background image which rounds off the whole mood.
Their message, the text font and the image must be consistent and the Image is to say more than a thousand words, the picture alone and flourishes font should produce a longing and a desire in the viewer.

Sell desires and then the price is a minor matter!
People are happy for their heart's desires and longings deeper into the Grab bag because they want to feel good and they satisfy their desires want.

Watch couples who marry there shall planned for months and everything should possible to be perfect, because it is ultimately the best day in the life of this two persons.
A white carriage drawn by white horses pulling the team as possible, a beautiful white wedding dress, white baptisms are released and the heaven ascend, etc.
These couples are happy to let cost be ready this day something, because it is everything to be perfect and some people have set themselves the goal of such people achieve their desires to help, the profession of wedding planner.
A wedding planner does nothing other than that he is trying the wishes of its convert the customer into action, he or she fulfill wishes and aspirations of People, for the people who come to them, expect exactly that they their wishes and desires get satisfied.
So give the people what you want and put yourself in their shoes.

Or ask yourself, what wishes and desires I have and you wish that someone satisfy these desires and longings can.
And if you know where and who will help you ensure that your wishes and aspirations into tangible reality, then do not hesitate long and book the weekend or the Cruise or the seminar - or whatever your wish is.
And you wonder also not great for the price, because this is a minor matter.

We remember so again on the following facts:
People have desires and dreams and they are looking for people or ways that will help them to realize this.

What matters is only the result is always (wish longing fulfilled get)
and nothing else

Personal notes and implementation points:

1. _____

_____

_____

2. _____

_____

_____

3. _____

_____

_____

4. _____

_____

_____

5. _____

_____

_____

Provide service - day in, day out!

As an attentive reader and reader you will certainly not have escaped your attention that I write a lot about customer service and yes, you have the absolute right detected.
For this is the be all and that's why I stress this so often, I mention it not because I knew nothing else to write for you, but that you of this fact are very aware.

A good customer service is to your business, a kind of life insurance in Entrepreneurial field.

What we mean by a good customer service?
When we tell a guest or caller that we his request and concerns only need to clarify and call him on the same day or the next day - then we also call on the same or next day!

When we tell a prospect on the phone or by mail, that we our Still send out documentation by mail - please send it also on this day out!
Customers and guests appreciate a first class service, and they are also happy it willing to let this cost anything even if your prices are higher as the competitor, if the guest knows here agrees with the service and I can leave me that everything is organized to my satisfaction, then pay it gladly a higher price.

Customers appreciate an excellent service and I will in the chapter for what do you and your company in the public to know, then you make sure that your house is known for an excellent service.
And this they can also cost a bit.
If you are thinking now, this type of service and customer courtesy to the guest is just for the big 4 or 5 star hotels, then I have to disappoint you.
Guests and customers appreciate good customer service anywhere in the world because it does not matter whether neighborhood restaurant or posh hotel.
Or do you expect when you go to a "normal" restaurant, that you a cold coffee or served a cold lunch, where you then to himself can say, "oh it was just only a normal restaurant and since I can not expect more! "
No, certainly not, you can expect the same great service in a restaurant.

After all, customer-oriented thinking and service readiness is not a question of a seal of approval, but a personal internal commitment and Readiness.

As a restaurateur, you live it that people come to you and your offer services in the form of food and drink to third parties and thus do not come even past the sale.
No matter if you "only" reinschaut a passerby of a cup of coffee with you or whether it is a wedding with all the trimmings worth several thousand dollars or pounds is.

People expect that you will get with you what you imagine a delicious hot cappuccino or a multi-course wedding menu with several courses, fine wine and beautiful decorated tables.
You sell yourself and your business, whether consciously or unconsciously, while also it does not matter whether it is your car or to insurance companies or in Case comes to eating or drinking, the principle is always the same, people come to you with a clear idea what you want.

You need to sell every day!
If your operation of an industrial society is one, then you need your ideas for new investments or acquisitions or whatever, the Board of Directors sell so this agrees and gives his blessing to the planned projects.
Or do you want to go away on holiday, you want to go to the mountains during your partners prefer it prefers to sunbathe on the beach!
So if you want that your partner comes along in the mountains and his idea of the gives up the sun and the beach in your favor, you need only hear your partner from the convincing advantages of a holiday in the mountains, give him or her so your idea sale.

You will now may argue that this is not comparable with the a car salesman or an insurance agent!
True, the product or service is different, but the principle remains basically the same, namely, the advantages and benefits of its service or product to the man, resp. to bring the woman.
And so we come to the conclusion that in a counselor like this a few words on the subject of sale should be addressed.
Stop, do not worry now, this is not how - do - I - more - sales - on - my - Cart treatise, but if we look carefully, so bear this book entitled "From guests to friends" and when we made our guests want to make friends, then we need this from us and our services also convinced.
Even friends want to benefit are in their and our relationship, because who calls another person a friend when this connection a more trouble than joy it brings - I think none of us, and it also establishes not, right?

If you make good friends from your guests, well, then, you and your staff did a good job and offer a good service.
And that is what, in effect, to make new friends and have a good this service to provide our friends and that we deliver our service to that our guests never come up with the idea to another restaurant to switch.
You are in good hands with you and so it should stay in the future.

A few little tips at this point for a successful communication with your guests:

If you go to the table where guests are just the food, then you say not, are you satisfied or does it taste?
Say instead, "Is everything to your complete satisfaction or you have a wish? "
Such a statement sounds also very different.

When guests come to a restaurant to eat at you, then they welcome with a handshake and the following words:
"You have made an excellent choice, for which I congratulate you needs. "
I know you will patronize our food and be sure to join us feel good. "
Here you can still sit on an icing on the cake top by three two enumerate specialties prepared by the chef only today evening:
"Our chef has for tonight something very special for thought of our guests, like fish / beef etc. .... "

Or someone has booked an event with you, a celebration or Birthday party, you could host the birthday child and the host salute with the following words:
"Congratulations on your birthday / family reunion / company party Mr. Meyer, and I assure you, you are a very beautiful tonight experience in our house hard and pleasant hours.
You are a great boss / father / father-in-itself as to the Welfare of his children / staff cares. "

This should serve as inspiration as you receive your guests in and You also see it here, make it different from the masses and show your guests to an open friendly attitude that you are happy to have tonight or lunch at your restaurant.

If you have hotel rooms, then put a hand-written card to the pillow of your guests, I emphasize hand-written in the following words:
"I thank you for your good choice to stay at our home and wish you for the duration of your stay a beautiful and pleasant Time. "
Kind regards, Yours, Hans Huber and his team.
Signing you in person the card or if this is not possible, then make sure that your deputy takes care of - but do it in each guest without exception!

After the occasion or celebration, is prior to the event or celebration!

If hot, you take after!
The occasion or the celebration is over, everyone was happy and satisfied and everything worked perfectly, congratulations, very well done and kudos to all Involved.
But that's not the story ends!
In all cases, you say, yes that was a great evening and all were happy and satisfied, now the guests are gone and I think you will come back?
You think and want it to be, but surely you are not that fact?
So help after appropriately by doing the following.

Call the organizer one, no later than two days after the event to (his phone number so hopefully you have not) and would like to thank again for his visit and that it was you and your home a pleasure to be able to carry out the event and let him know that you've been to now looking forward to welcoming you soon it back in your plant.

Here it goes again to the psychological aspect.
Imagine you had and an event in a hotel or restaurant one or two days later you receive a call from the owner or director himself, of thanking you!
How do you feel since?
You will certainly think, "Oh wow, but that is attentive, something I have never seen and that's real customer service what this man or this woman makes. "
And yes, this is real and you are in your guest a positive memory remain, such a call lasts about two minutes, and these two minutes are very well spent.
But even in this case, the slogan is true, do it without exception.

This method can also apply for a guest of yours holidays had made or just a night stayed long, surprise your guests with a spontaneous phone call, they will rejoice and be happy stay with you again when you are back in your area.
Explore new and creative ways and you will see the reactions not be long in coming.

You keep it all for far too time consuming and too exaggerated?
Not at all dear reader, for you to do things that do not do their competitors and this is exactly what differentiates you from the competition.

And again a set you should remember well!

*Successful people are so successful,
because you do things that unsuccessful people do not do that.*

Personal notes and implementation points:

1. _____

_____

_____

2. _____

_____

_____

3. _____

_____

_____

4. _____

_____

_____

5. _____

_____

_____

Side issues still relevant

There are a number of things for many caterers in your eyes a represent minor point, but in reality there are no side issues, but is aware of the guests or unconsciously perceived.

The theme of the environment!
I have already visited restaurants that had something of a fairground itself, colorful jumbled umbrellas, the same image at the pillows and tablecloths, a mess.
Nothing against advertising on the umbrellas, but those should be at least be uniform, ie, all from the same supplier.
Same goes for the cushions on the seats, look there, too, that there is a order prevails.
The tablecloths when you put tablecloths on the tables, then show all tables with tablecloths and not just isolated to a few tables.
I once asked a waitress why the tables are not covered back there, include some not to your company?
The answer to the waitress, however, but since there is rarely someone sitting there, we place no tablecloths on these tables!
Aha, I thought to myself, no wonder no one ever sits there because these tables screaming yes begs dear guest not sit so our part of horticulture, our Corner is so unfriendly and impersonal, because you have me simply uncomfortable rather feel guest!

The theme of the menu box!
In many companies, you will see a menu box somewhere on the facade attached, where food and drinks are touted.
There is nothing wrong and a guest can find out in advance about the offer.
But many times I've seen these menu boxes indulge in a miserable existence had to, because no one really cared about them.
The daily menu was replaced a year ago, the last time the sight glass was dirty and filthy and around the entire box around gathered at the cobwebs.
Keep your menu box in order and if it no longer need, you probably should consider to take him away.

The theme of the plants!
Here, too often a sad picture emerges in either the overgrown garden wildly to himself or potted plants have withered and faded.
Also here you should definitely create order, the flowers boxes with the withered crops you create better from the field of view of your guests and the Plants in the garden, you should throw an eye.
It does not mean that you have to do everything yourself, you determine a person which is responsible for all these things.
Another variant would be how I did it:

Hire a pensioner where it is fun to independently around the Environment to care.
Agree with him a certain amount and a number of hours he or they can be divided free to move around plants, the menu box and other little things that no one else cares for the operation really has time.
So you have the peace of mind that someone cares about and you have time
to take care of your guests and customers.

I know, especially smaller businesses forget the points raised happy or they tell themselves that this is not so important appears - in your eyes!
But it does not matter if you can see the operation of your own eyes, important to see your business from the eyes of the guest is and how this our company is responsible.

Let's make the following thought experiment dear reader and dear reader:
Suppose you are planning a birthday party and visit now various local of which you think that these might be for your party in question?
Now drive to the parking lot and get out, it offers itself to you the following image:
The garden is overgrown, in the box menu, you can hardly read anything, because the sight glass so dirty and full of spin honeycomb.
They go on to have a third of the tables on the terrace neither a tablecloth or seat cushions on the chairs, do you still see half rolled garden hose attached to a faucet.
The umbrellas are a motley collection of suppliers of the innkeeper, lying on the ground everywhere cigarette butts and other debris around, with a broom was long gone wiped here!

So what is your first impression of this restaurant?
Not the best and you are seriously considering, I should here my celebration organize, everything looks so dirty and messy?
The host and the waitress may be lovely people and the host can determined very good cook, but still you have decided, no, this I do my celebration definitely not!

Always remember a fact!
For the first impression, there is no second chance.

It is the first impression of a visitor gets of your company and due which he will make a first impression very quickly.
As I said, You may be a nice guy and the waitress or the waiter very friendly for you to make very much offset, but the impression which the guest has won (especially if it is a new guest) will remain.
He will drink from you, and maybe some coffee, but a rise in Carry you or even a friend to his friends and acquaintances, it is not likely.

And what applies to outside, also applies to the tavern itself.

How does it look?
I've been to a restaurant where all the windowsills with soft toys packed were, or the owner had a soft spot for whales on the walls hung pictures down of whales, even hung from the ceiling and several Perpetomobile in this operation were next to the cash register at the local beverages and in various niches distributed plush whales and erected.

Again, I like to treat each his liking, but must the host or the landlady not expect from me that I or other guests of this wide willingly with her share.
It is also not wrong to try a pleasant cozy atmosphere in the to create a restaurant, but it is also different.

If you value the fact that flowers are on the table, then ensure that there are fresh flowers and, otherwise leave no cheap junk Far East It stay rather you gain by much more.

And the loo?
Not for nothing it is said, the toilet is the calling card of the house, it is there clean, then is found cleanliness and cleanliness in the rest of the house.
In the meantime many companies you can create a so-called "clean table" see, that is, as is to be read when purified, at what time and abbreviation of the employee.
However, in many companies, this also seems to be only a token exercise to say, look here, we pay attention to how our toilets look like!
More than once I have seen that according to this "clean table" before five or ten minutes should have been cleaned, but the Paper towel dispenser was empty, or it had no toilet paper.
I do not think one or two roles in five or ten minutes Toilet paper and were consumed during this period also allegedly (according to Table) filled paper towel dispenser is already empty again!
Again, paper is patient or in other words, trust is good, control is better.

The greed-is-cool method misunderstood and interpreted!

Economy and efficiency are two important factors when it comes to survival of a company going, but here save many caterers unfortunately on wrong place, which eventually turns out to be negative illusion shot.
Let me give you a few examples:
I was a bar with a garish neon lighting.
On the whole length of the cylinder Bartresens beautiful candles were placed in just such a beautiful candlesticks.
I and my company asked the barmaid if perhaps the neon light could dampen something and to create a more intimate atmosphere, even the beautiful could light candles?
Her answer, we can not regulate the neon light and unfortunately what the candles concerns, which are decorative and not intended for kindling.
Then she added, that would not be profitable if they constantly new cylinder would have to buy candles.

I and my companion have replied nothing on this answer why also, she wanted to show her guests that she has beautiful candles but that these are only for viewing and not intended for kindling!
Had the good lady, the bright neon lights all identified and only the lighted candles, there would have been a very different atmosphere in the restaurant, but it is, some people can not teach themselves.

A similar example I experienced in a restaurant, which were also candles on the table and I asked him if we could light the candle, said the waitress, no, do not want our boss that are more intended for decoration.

If you repent as Throw the few euros or Swiss francs for candles, then make just no candles on the tables, because such statements make hosts only questionable, because it is saved in the wrong place on your guests.

Another example, again had in a bar, the owner of an expensive system installed with beamer and wheeled down a big screen.
But only very rarely he let down the big screen, because in this projector would have a lamp and this lamp would only approximately 1000 hours of operation hold before he had to replace it again.
And so a lamp, he explained further on, it would cost a few hundred dollars.
But the same host had no trouble hundred francs in useless advertising invest.
Again, it is often saved in the wrong place and it is in the sum of all these things that make a difference whether people like coming in the operation or not and whether they will ever come back after their first visit!

As in the case of Candles and beamer for some restaurateurs like this banal his examples, but exactly these mundane things make it out just as well as the first impression a guest gets the already outside when he takes on the parking runs.
It must be coherent to Z (leaving the organization) of A (arrival), a appealing picture from outside as well as inside, friendly staff which happy and like to host, a chief of the guests by name (if he knows) is responsive and gives them the hand.

That would be a bit like when someone buys a stove but this never used because he is afraid that thing cost me yes electricity or gas.
If you buy something, then use this appropriate thing or object too and if not (for whatever reason do not) then let it prefers to remain the same.

As I said, economy in honor, but used in the wrong place it does the opposite.

Personal notes and implementation points:

1. _____

   _____

   _____

2. _____

   _____

   _____

3. _____

   _____

   _____

4. _____

   _____

   _____

5. _____

   _____

   _____

The employee has the word

The employee has the word and the chief technology it!
In this chapter I want more detail on that topic motivation because Motivation is the driving force behind our actions and also provides us with the motivation that cause us to do something or not to do.
Employees and motivation is always an issue for managers when a supervisor or boss is not able to motivate his staff he will always be alone on a limb and are pulling the hair and ask these thankless dissatisfied pack and he will have the feeling that all the have conspired operation against him.
Now we come to speak on the topic of leadership!
Anyone who knows working with other people, or at least has had the experience that everyone has their little quirks and Spleene.
And every person has certain skills and talents, some of these known or unknown and the better someone according to his ability can work, the better the results will show it.

Each behavior is based on a motivation and thought.
I'm doing this right now, or later, should I call them now or should I let it be, etc.
All the time people are busy with their thoughts and their inner dialogues they carry with themselves, now I do this or that, should I or should I not.
And because of our inner thoughts and impulses we decide then to act.

All well and good you are now thinking - but how do I know the skills and talents of my staff?
And what do I do if my employee his own skills and talents does not know himself?
Do I now need to be a therapist or NLP Coach?
The question is, how do I use this information for me and how can I apply them to achieve the desired results!

No, you do not need (if you have the appropriate training is the advantage) and I will give you a few helpful tips at hand, as you find out where the skills and talents with the individual employees lie, and even with yourself!
What do you like to do and what you enjoy doing and what you would do, even if you would get no money for it, just do it because it gives you a makes such a fun and flourish properly in this activity?
Is there such a job for you

Motivate people in two ways!
1 You want something that you have not yet!
2 You want something not that you have!

In practice, it looks like this:
Mr. X has to keep the dream his own restaurant to be his own boss (Mr. X so wants something that he has not, his own restaurant).

Mr. X has come trouble making ends meet because his restaurant is not running and he makes little revenue to cover its running costs (Mr. X wants more visitors and more revenue to ensure its operation profitable again and the black writes).

In the first example, Lord desires because he be his own boss X is a restaurant wants, so he wants a restoration operation which he has not yet.
His motivation is; towards a restaurant.

In the second example, Mr. X wants more visitors and therefore more sales, thus his dire financial situation improved again, in this case, he has to little guests and sales, he do not want this anymore, he wants to get away from.
His motivation is, away from the lousy sales - and visitor numbers to more sales and more guests.

In all walks of life it's all about these two types of motivation, either to something or away from something away.

> Towards better health, away from disease and lethargy
> Towards a harmonious relationship, away from the single life.
> Towards inner peace and serenity, away from the hustle and bustle.

I have spoken to you of this principle in earlier chapters, people want something that they have not or not yet and they want something not that they have.
It is very crucial that a leader of these two types of motivation is aware, because this knowledge and knowledge spans all Areas and areas of life, it refers not only to the professional life.
You can be happy and content in a job with the type of activity that you do every day, but privacy in a disharmonious relationship that you very stressed and will not give any real benefit.

My tip: it gets worse ever, you separate.
I know in such matters always plays the emotional closeness to the relevant person an important role, which is the same as a friend who works for you and which you know that you have to part with him or her because he your business more harm than good.
But even here, you are just aware of it gets worse as it never already, you can try having a conversation, but if you already have had several meetings and the situation has not improved, then have you (as hard as it sometimes is) act and the necessary steps companies.
Because the longer you wait, the worse it will be and is you task at hand or the conversation heavy on the stomach.

Me. the author is clear that such matters are not always easy, no matter if there is a termination for an employee, a difficult talk with your partner or business partner, but certain things demand of us that we remain steadfast.
And life is not a football game with second round.

Let us now look at how you can change the motivation of themselves and may increase, and how to influence the motivation of your employees can you not interested, right?

How do you motivate yourself?
Come only when you stand in the aisles with his back to the wall, So only the bull by the horns is possible only salvation?

This can happen if someone smokes so much that he breathing difficulties and has a smoker's cough and that person knows, if I do not change now then I am in a year or even earlier dead or incapacitated!
So the moment the person will realize that they must change something and so can not go there.

In this case, it is a way of motivation, the person wants to smoke-free be and protect their health, the so-called pain threshold is reached, the point where the person says, now an end to that!
What can a person do in this case, she wants to quit smoking, but brings it's just not ready to get away from the cigarette and the nicotine?
First, the person must consider what they substitute for smoking could use, for example, they could stand up a mental picture of yourself stand up as it stands beaming happy and full of energy.
And exactly this state will reach the person also, because this is what they wishes, away from the smokers cough and difficulty breathing, go to vitality and energy.

I want you here now a technique from NLP (neuro linguistic programming) imagine you can use to change this and other undesirable conditions.

This technique is called the Swish Pattern:

1 First, determine the specific behavior that you want to use, in our case, this is smoking. You can also watch a situation introduce and select where you would like certain people to certain want to be and circumstances in life.

2 Treat this limitation as a power, you say thank you that You have smoked and will now get rid of it, or that you are now certain in certain situations. How do you know that you have the behavior or the problem. Which are the triggers that at It pulse is triggered, what have you thought or made or what happened when they decided to grab for a cigarette and a cigarette smoke. Imagine, you would need someone your explain and teach behavior and its triggers - what would this Person can make.
There must always be a reason or impulse, a certain stimulus, the the reaction triggers. When this trigger is internally and mentally produced is, you make it an image exactly as you see it. Someone has annoyed and now you need a cigarette so as to relax, or you have just been completed, now drink your coffee and to smoke a cigarette, just as you for always after eating Coffee smoking a cigarette. Or could be the trigger that during You're on the phone and make calls, smoke on the side.

3 Find visual images trigger your behavior, you will be annoyed and taking up smoking, you make phone calls and smoke it at the same time, or what whatever the trigger is that you smoke.
If you look carefully and deal with it, you will always find a trigger, something that has caused you to start smoking have resorted.
Vary around with it until it's true for you and you appropriate the Have found trigger, then think of something else before you the practice to continue.

4 Now think about how you want to be really vital and smoke-free, or how would people who would not have these limitations by Smoking (difficulty breathing smoker's cough). How would you describe yourself see if you have achieved these desired changes?
They would have more opportunities would be efficient, you'd be the man similarly you would like to be.
It should be an idea, a picture of yourself with the desired Qualities, without the specific behavior, in our example, smoking.
The image must be attractive and motivating effect on you, this your picture future selves.
Then check whether the new image fits to you and whether it ecologically is, ie, agrees with it in line with your values and beliefs and is it is also voices for the environment and people.
Now think of the possibilities with this new self-portrait have, free breathing, wellbeing and all other positive aspects of the be related.
Make sure that the new self-image is enticing enough so that you are motivated to carry out the new changes, you will need this new behavior really want and be amazed.
Now you also interrupt this state and think of something else, to your pet or to the last holiday.

5 Now take the picture from the first step, in our case, the image from smoking and make it big and clear. In the lower left corner or right to make a small dark picture of your new desired behavior to be vital and non-smoking.
Now take the image you want to use, you big and bright have made and let it quickly become smaller and the move the background while you simultaneously right the small image in the leave or left corner appear big and bright.
An old picture of you make lightning-fast small and the image of the new behavior
quickly large, to gain at this exercise, you can either snap your fingers while you perform this change or can a word like Schwupps or use smudge, what for you fits better and is more effective.
After you have done this exercise once, ask yourself mentally a neutral white screen in front, then repeat this exercise yet four consecutive times - image of old behavior large and clear, the new desirable behavior in the small left or right corner of the great Image, then you say the right word for you or snap your fingers and replace the two images from a flash mentally.
Make after each pass your inner mental screen again freely by you imagine a white neutral canvas.

If you notice no change after five attempts, then make Do not continue if something does not work, then you have something and you should do something else.
Be creative in this case, maybe you need a new picture of your new desirable behavior add more intensity, perhaps you need to make it bigger and brighter, because a large radiant image has more intensity than a small colorless image

6 If you are satisfied after these two passages, so you are now testing the result and think of the shutter has been led to you have resorted to cigarette. It still causes the same response, that is to say, you still have to grab the craving for a cigarette?
If you are the next time this situation, look for the new Situation out, so how do you want to be now.
Snap your fingers or say your word like Schwupps or smudge and feel in this new desirable state and let the cigarette stay.
This technique can affect many areas of your personal life apply, they work quickly and effectively and this technique also shows that you can change a direction quickly - without great pain or hardships.

When you snap your fingers and immediately come to the desired state, then you have done the exercise with success, because in this exercise is about to acquire a new behavior.
And through this new behavior, you also have other choices available and this change your thoughts and Empfindngen that you can steer in the desired direction.

I wish you great results with this simple yet very effective technique, I've been using the same method already some changes quickly brought about and you can too.
The more often you do this exercise, the better you will be in it and the better effective and also the desired changes will look.

And now we talk about how you motivate your employees as an executive can, a topic that interested each supervisor and what like a book this also should not be missed.
Do not you dear reader?

What motivates people and why is motivation important?

The motivation consultant and bestselling author Anthony Robbins once said:
"There are two things that motivate people to success, inspiration and despair. "
Furthermore you have already read above, people want something you not have or they do not want anything more, they have.
Big goals and dreams motivate people to excel, the prospect on a date with the person of your dreams can be very motivating.
The view to the post of Chairman of the Board can be very tempting be motivating and, of building a successful restaurant can be very be motivating that someone inside kneels and gives everything he has.

I am of the opinion that a person can only realize its true potential when it is burning inside for his ideas.

And each of us has very special talents and abilities and we should bring this to fruition in order to lead a real rich and fulfilling life.
It can also be motivating, more self-confidence and self-esteem to gain more to become the person and to be that you would have liked. So you see, there are dozens of reasons why people motivate because each of us his own desires and goals in life that he or she realize and wants to realize

Each of us can even find out what kind he motivates himself, he wants something away, we come into action only when we almost on the brink want to stand and protect us from the threat of back stay and save, then we are due to the determined away from motivation strategy.
Or he enthuses by its desires and goals and are all, no one must motivate him only because he knows himself what he wants and goes directly way towards it, then such a person is due to the motivation towards out strategy,
If you are asking yourself if something is wrong with me because I have a way of motivated am, I can assure you, none of the two strategies is better or worse
than the other.
It always depends on the corresponding circumstance and situation, even a way to motivated person can develop a way of motivation in disease.

If we ourselves can not motivate us for one thing, then it will be difficult for us to motivate another person for one thing or task.

An off strategy is also required in certain occupations and compelling:
An accountant needs to work very diligently with the numbers and away from strategy have to create a clean accounting.
Just as a lecturer must apply one way of spelling mistakes Strategy by a manuscript get added correctly.

So we come to the employees and their motivation!

Again, have employees, just like other people, these two types to motivate yourself, either on something or from something away.
We realize how a person talks to us, she always speaks only of Problems we are dealing with a person who is away from motivated, because, she sees problems and want to get away from these problems.
An employee comes to you and tells you, I want the best waiter or be employee of the month, then he is towards motivated, he has a clear objective and he also tells you.
On the way someone speaks to us, we recognize the motivation direction, so be sure to like people and talk to you.

So how do you motivate the two types of employees and what you need look for?

You may be wondering, goodness gracious, now I give him or her a salary increase and offer him else remuneration to him and this seems or they do not seem to care what kind of ungrateful man?

This man and the employee is not ungrateful, just for this employee important that you are pleased with him and praise him and he feels at you to have a safe workplace.

Such a person can not necessarily motivate with money and gifts than with praise and recognition.
What does that mean in practice?

Suppose that you envision for your team assembled and announce that you are planning a special occasion, let's say you are planning an entry into the Guinness Book of Records.

Now, those who are motivated him to say, wow cool and then could we still .... and those who are away from motivated, would only times worry about what could go wrong or where problems arise could and would be manifestations of the kind, you have considered this and that boss and there I still see a problem!

The best way to then two groups, those which it can be motivated by your workforce to worry what else you could offer and whether we are inside or outside carry the occasion.
Those employees who are motivated away from, now remain only once passive and consider then, after being ratified by the motivated towards ideas and suggestions have received ideas about what to do if any problems would show up and how they can be solved.
So you see, take care of the one design a battle plan and the other located behind solutions to problems and to have a plan B if this needs to be of should.

The way how the different staff will respond to your statement shows you the motivational direction of the employees.
Those who are excited and already beginning the wildest ideas to develop and those who respond behave and make already about possible difficulties thoughts.
But neither of the two strategies is better or worse than the other.
It just shows their motivational strategy, towards or away from, that's all.

A much more useful and productive point of view is away from motivation is to understand them as away from problems.
Many people are prone to this type of motivation, are excellent problem solver, have their language betrays this, because they come to you and say you; boss, there's a problem, because when you see the problem must you solve it.
After solving a particularly serious problem these people feel an emotional relaxation and have a personal AHA experience.
People with a way to move on motivation goals and you can this seen also in their mode of expression, saying phrases like; My goal is to to be successful and to make the best sales and be recognized.
If this category of people get closer to their goals, they experience a emotional exhilaration, an inner Yes.

Once more:

So pay attention to the way in which people express themselves to recognize and find out on which way the person concerned motivated, either toward or away from.

And now, a word on the subject of communication at this point.

As a chief, you enter each day other people instructions and expect this you also receive instructions.
If you want your employees just execute your instructions as you imagine that, then you always say first what you want and do not last what you want.
For a better understanding of this point is an example:

"This time we want to make sure that in time for the banquet, the cold buffet is constructed before the first guests enter the room, So please before exactly consider what to put where and no more delay at the last minute, okay?"

"This time, think carefully about where something is set up at the cold buffet for the banquet and that we are ready in time to set up before the first guests to the hall entered. So we are on schedule and have no stress, okay?"

It is exactly the same sentence, but in a different order!

Which of the above two sets of positive affect on you?
The first example is said first what should be the goal, and then click the problem pointed out what you want to avoid.
The second example is first addressed the problem (construction of the buffets and the timely completion) and what you want to avoid and it is drawn, what is the goal (no stress and in time).

The second example is therefore well received by the employees because he that being said what you do not want them and then pretending to be what should be the goal and what you expect of them and wish.
Because people only ever remembered what they last communicated was, it is important that you last say always what you expect and what should be the goal.

This principle can also be applied to other areas, for example in a telephone call or a job interview, you always mention first what you do not want and which should be avoided, and finally, what you want and what is the goal.

**Thereby you can remain in good memory and people come to your Wishes and requirements of.
Look in the future for this crucial difference in your communication with employees and your environment, and you will notice that people respond positively and what's even better, your instructions are carried out and discharged as desired.**

Personal notes and implementation points:

1. _____

_____

_____

2. _____

_____

_____

3. _____

_____

_____

4. _____

_____

_____

5. _____

_____

_____

Let's summarize!

A good relationship with guests, employees and our environment is not witchcraft, but rather an understanding of the interrelationships of the right intercourse each other.
I compare the life always with a puzzle or a Combination of numbers in a vault.
Just like a jigsaw puzzle, one first has no clear view because it is so many different parts are, a clear picture, the more yields with time but Parts fit together and the more advanced the image is.
Or the combination in a safe when the correct combination known, then it is easy to open the safe and to its coveted content come, we do not however know the combination, so we can try and practice as long as we want, the safe will not open and the contents of which we so much desire is denied us.

With our fellow human beings is like the a safe's combination, know we have the right combination, we have wonderful access to other people and are able to lead a harmonious relationship with them based on mutual respect and appreciation.
Often it does not take much and we have set the right combination and find the wire and access to our employees, guests and fellow human beings and from my personal work as a caterer and a coach, I know that one of the exciting tasks is to work with people, because each of us differently ticking.
But with the right tools and the right knowledge I can access created for every human being and build, it just needs a little understanding and knowledge of the people, his motives and his story.
Let's start to care about the other person and we take part in its history, just as each of us has his own story and we find out what drives these people and what the reasons are that he or she does what they do.

The Indian proverb fits in this context very well here and explains everything you need:
"In order to judge another person, you must first thousand walk miles in his moccasins "

Dale Carnegie and Napoleon Hill to describe this wonderful in their classic bestsellers very well, show interest in the people around them, what these people have to say.
If we make it, a sincere interest in appreciation and respect apply towards other people, then this will not only help yourself, but you do with the world and humanity in general a large service.
This is not to write about any theological treatise, but all these points belong to it, if it comes to that you true to the book title from your guests make your friends.

And you've also noticed that it and for a good relationship with the host customers do not need so much, it is the one important ingredients such as at a Number combination of a safe and if you know this, then opens you a new wonderful world.
This book does not intend to be a standard work or to be, me, the author is clear that there is a need for commitment and the will, every day a special day to make.

As a restaurateur and hotelier you are dealing with people and the word operation contains the verb "serve", so someone else a service to prove.
So we prove our guests and visitors of our services by you openly and warmly welcome us he and his guests and friends our Appreciation and thanks are making of the he expects from us.
Because we want from him for his hard-earned money and we are a service companies, so we provide what is desired and demanded.

Today, ideas and creativity are needed and in the catering we have any Lot of ways to implement ideas so our visitors and guests an experience to offer.

Enter what these people want and make sure that you have contributed with their actions to make them feel a little better.
People will thank you and love to come back again and again, because with you it makes you fun and joy to spend time and at precisely these moments they remember always happy.
The people had come to you maybe having a bad day, so make sure that people feel good and can put their negative feelings in order to replenish your energy with you.
And in order to offer guests an experience it can often needs, as in the have read this book, often not too much to the wishes to be and expectations.
Much has been made by your guests the necessary attention have placed, they warmly welcomed and say goodbye.
Kindness and attention are virtues in our fast-paced and in the hustle and bustle of everyday life go like to forget about it and appreciate People even more so when you look at a host or a hotel owner himself of these virtues is again aware of and alive.

Much of what you have read in this small counselor can be rapidly and without put a lot of effort, but - you have to do it, every day - it is the essences for a good and fruitful guest loyalty.
And to top it is also to a fruitful relationship and loyalty to our Guests so that they always like to come to us and also their guests and my friends.
Because if you do not do it, it is another to do on your behalf and for its Efforts will be rewarded, your competitors do not sleep!

I myself have found in my years of working as a host again that these methods of which I reported to you and tells in this book, function.
Because, whether hotel or restaurant or fast food, it's all about people and their needs for recognition and esteem in which Infrastructure and the location may be different, but the principle remains the same.
And remember, if a system works in one place, then it works the same at a different location.
This can be very well observed in the catering business, the base and the products remain the same, everything is what changes the employee and the various locations.

And if they have worked in my plants, why should they not work at their factory.

Or, as we have seen the example of Luxemburgerli at Sprüngli, this be sold and shipped anywhere in the world beyond, people around the globe love good quality products and are prepared to pay the appropriate price to pay.
Or, as we have seen from the philosophy of Steve Jobs, if we help other people to achieve their goals and desires, you will wide support us willingly, our services and products.

Or as we have seen, there are little touches which ensure that we stay with our fellow human beings in good memory, a hand-written welcome card on the bed of the guest in his room.
A welcome drink is on the house of the personal address with pre and last name.
A relationship between two people is like a plant, so that they grow and can thrive, it requires the necessary fertilizer and as a plant light and water needs so that they can grow and thrive, need human relations also light and water in the form of attention and appreciation.
These conditions are essential, you neglect they will give you the Guests and fail to look for a restaurant or hotel, where these conditions are met to their expectations.

I hope you open this book a few important ideas to have given way to may and wish you, your employees and Guests a great and inspiring for all pages long lasting bond.
If you take the advice mentioned in this book to heart and implement and apply them consistently, I'm sure, yes I'm even assume confident that you will after a short time a noticeable change in your will find guests and employees.
Let us remember again the purpose of this book, cookery programs and Cookbooks abound, but rarely will you find a guide how to get out guests makes friends of the house.
And as I've noticed because of my observations and research, it is a concern of many guests and also from the caterers, a to have such a counselor at hand.
I have the book and therefore written to help restaurant owners going to do with identity and creativity more out of the existing possibilities, and because I like to pass on my knowledge and when I see that circumstances have thanks to me positively improved, then I am pleased, huge.
It pleases me not for me but for the people or the company are the these positive changes have succeeded.
For what I want for me, I also wish other, a long happy fulfilling life and abundance in all areas.

After all, the image of the restaurant is in many places was injured and is not for best, some of the reasons I've tried to explain to you in this book.
It is not for the guests or the situation, I know Gastronomiebetriebe the are "off the beaten track" and yet they are very well attended and I know catering restaurants because you have to wait for lunch, if you are not reserved have!
If you now want to know how do these companies so that they be running up from their guests, the answers can be found in this small Book you are holding in your hands.
It's the little things, the little crucial things which these establishments do differently and bring them their success.

Make best the example yourself and visit a company in your surrounding area is well-known that it is going well.
Visit him and see what this operation, from the boss make their employees to ensure that the operation runs as good as is the appearance and hello?

**Success is no accident but the result of a particular action
and a certain inner state of mind.**

You will find that these companies (perhaps consciously or unconsciously) a most of the written down here points have been observed, and because their owners or manager is aware of what it is, a good relationship with his to have guests.
Give your guests an added value and thus a reason, just for you to come and not to another restaurant or hotel, what you offer, which he nowhere else gets.
And here we are again at the point and the question, what do you want and your operating be known?

Watch the market and the needs of your guests and offer and deliver you, because it plays the gratification where we are back to the point of the survey no matter what you want, but that what your guest wants, because he and only he brings you sales.

To close the circle at this point and complete the picture, stays at Conclusion as the quintessence of all this observations and findings left:

"What matters is the result and nothing else!"

Which countable result you want to achieve?

Personal notes and implementation points:

1. _____

_____

_____

2. _____

_____

_____

3. _____

_____

_____

4. _____

_____

_____

5. _____

_____

_____

To say remains dear reader ....

Now we are already at the end of my counselor.
I hope for you that you are doing some great insights and inspirations had and have already implemented one or the other point?

This guide can bring you a lot in your company and I wrote it with the intention and idea to give you here a practical and no theoetischen counselor at hand.
So I urge you to work your damt and put what you have learned into practice.
Look for yourself what you can make use of the tips and suggestions and put what you have learned into your everyday work.
Knowledge and skill by itself is useless unless you apply and implement what they have learned and I have written this book as a practical guide and not as a dust catcher for the bookshelf.

At the very end I want to give you a food for thought with along the way and if you are aware of which, your life will change quite formidable.

"That which we direct our focus determines our whole life."

"And that's what our focus, we will also experience."

"This in turn determines our feelings."

For yourself and your staffmembers and all guests, I wish your all the best in the future, realize other poeples desires and everyone will win the game, there are only winners.
And I think, this is the best intention you can do in your life, to take care that everyone wins the game and to be successful.
I wish you all the best my friend.

Sincerely.
Your Dominik Fritz Buri

About the Author

Dominik Fritz Buri born in 1963 in Stans in Nidwalden in Switzerland eorld came, grew up in Ennetbuergen.
After his apprenticeship as a cook in a traditional home-style restaurant, he completed additional training as a waiter and attended the hotelmanagement school Belvoirpark in Zurich.

He worked for several years as a manager in several food businesses and reorganized several years rundown gastronomy Businesses and they put on a sound economic basis.
Later he continued his education in the field of neuro-linguistic programmings short NLP called to his knowledge of human behavior and Deepen peak performance.
Today Dominik Fritz Buri gives his broad knowledge of professionals from the gastronomy further and advocates, catering to a better Light and prestige to help the public.

Is addition to his own personal column in the newspaper Happy Times online, he is the author of the book series circuit with frustration of its range there are now four volumes as well as an anthology & Workbook there, all available on Amazon are.

In addition, Fritz Buri Dominik still writes novels.

Fritz Buri Dominik now lives in Ennetburgen.

www.ingramcontent.com/pod-product-compliance
Lightning Source LLC
Chambersburg PA
CBHW081834170526
45167CB00007B/2805